T0169606

Do You Still Think GOD Is **Good?**

Do You Still Think GOD Is Good?

Candid conversations about
The Problem of Evil

Clayton
Brumby

NEW YORK

Do You Still Think GOD Is **Good?**

Candid conversations about The Problem of Evil

Published in New York, New York, by Morgan James Publishing. Morgan James and The Entrepreneurial Publisher are trademarks of Morgan James, LLC. www.MorganJamesPublishing.com

The Morgan James Speakers Group can bring authors to your live event. For more information or to book an event visit The Morgan James Speakers Group at www.TheMorganJamesSpeakersGroup.com.

All Scripture quotations, unless otherwise indicated, are from the New American Standard version of the Bible, Copyright 2006 MacArthur Study Bible, The Lockman Foundation, lockman.org

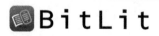

A FREE eBook edition is available
with the purchase of this print book

CLEARLY PRINT YOUR NAME IN THE BOX ABOVE

Instructions to claim your free eBook edition:
1. Download the BitLit app for Android or iOS
2. Write your name in UPPER CASE in the box
3. Use the BitLit app to submit a photo
4. Download your eBook to any device

ISBN 978-1-63047-065-4 paperback
ISBN 978-1-63047-066-1 eBook
ISBN 978-1-63047-067-8 hardcover
Library of Congress Control Number:
2013957035

Cover Design by:
Chris Treccani
www.3dogdesign.net

Interior Design by:
Bonnie Bushman
bonnie@caboodlegraphics.com

In an effort to support local communities, raise awareness and funds, Morgan James Publishing donates a percentage of all book sales for the life of each book to Habitat for Humanity Peninsula and Greater Williamsburg.

Get involved today, visit
www.MorganJamesBuilds.com.

Habitat
for Humanity®
Peninsula and
Greater Williamsburg
Building Partner

To Elizabeth.
Your love and friendship
are incalculable gifts to me.

Table of Contents

Preface

Two Challenges

The Christian gospel faces two challenges from the culture we want so badly to influence. The first is that posed by Darwinism and its attending philosophical underpinnings, metaphysical naturalism. In the minds of so many—if nature can do this without any input from God, then what's the deal?—God's role as creator vaporizes; He becomes irrelevant.

The second is perhaps even more direct. As the Christian message is proclaimed, it is increasingly met with the charge that the Judeo-Christian God is either inept, impotent or evil. How else can believers explain a world that's so out of control, so violent and painful and unfair? Thousands of children die of starvation and disease almost daily. Innocent people die in tornadoes and typhoons, earthquakes and tsunamis. This second question is known as "the problem of evil." The combination of these two issues creates a major traction problem for the gospel. In the minds of many, the Judeo-Christian God is evermore becoming a fairy tale.

Is this true? Is the gospel simply an anachronism? Something naïve people believed once upon a time, but that time has now passed? Hardly. Under close scrutiny neither of these challenges is up to the task of thwarting God's plan for this world—His plan for His people and His present and future kingdom. Why? When cross-examined, they themselves become vaporous.

This little book—*Do You Still Think God Is Good?*—addresses the second of these two challenges.

Neither of these issues is easy to confront. Investigating them takes courage and intelligence, study and spiritual fortitude. Those hostile to your faith—the "New Atheists" and their followers—are betting that this new generation of God's people, perhaps the last generation, is not up to the task. Not enough backbone, not enough smarts. You will determine if they are right. Walk away from these challenges as requiring too much, and they win. Pick up the arguments, wrestle with them until they're conquered, and you win. In fact, we all do.

The decision is yours. I hope you choose the latter.

Clayton Brumby
Sarasota, Florida

Chapter One

It Always Begins with a Question

"Okay, Fly-boy. Here's one for you."

Fly-boy. Eric winced. But it was a nickname Todd seemed determined to have stick.

"I'm not trying to start anything with this, okay?" Todd continued, sincerely. "We've covered this ground before, you know—you and God and all—and we probably will again. And I'm good with you believing what you believe—your choice."

Eric nodded as he folded his hands in his lap and leaned back in the desk chair, showing Todd he was taking him seriously and that he had his full attention.

"It's from a book called *The Pony Fish's Glow,*" Todd continued. "It's for a philosophy paper I have to write. The author is a professor named George Williams. He taught at the State University of New York. And he said here that this California anthropologist—well, let me just read you the quote:

> [California anthropologist Sarah Hrdy] studied a population of monkeys, *Hanuman langurs,* in northern India. Their mating system is what biologists call *harem polygyny*: dominant males have exclusive sexual access to a group of adult females, as long as they can keep other males away. Sooner or later, a stronger male usurps the harem and the defeated one must join the ranks of celibate outcasts. The new male shows his love for his new wives by trying to kill their unweaned infants. For each successful killing, a mother soon stops lactating and goes into estrous. . . . Deprived of her nursing baby, a female soon starts ovulating. She accepts the advances of her baby's murderer, and he becomes the father of her next child.
>
> Do you still think God is good?[1]

Todd looked up at Eric with raised eyebrows as a way of putting the ball in his court.

Eric grew thoughtful. Through other conversations he'd had with Todd, he knew this was a crucial question for his roommate. Todd had experienced some raw things in his nineteen years, and this kind of thing was no small issue for him.

Eric shrugged and laughed quietly. "I wouldn't have a clue as to where to begin with a question like that." But then something

---

1   George C. Williams, *The Pony Fish's Glow*, New York, BasicBooks, 1997, pp. 156-157.

occurred to him, and he glanced at his watch. "But I have a friend who might, and this is just the kind of question he loves. It's early enough. Why don't we give him a call?"

Todd agreed, and the call was made.

"Mike Murphy!" Eric grinned when he heard his friend's voice.

"Eric Jennings!" Mike exclaimed. It had been months since they'd last talked. "Wuzzup??!"

Eric laughed. Mike was in a light mood.

"My roommate has just asked me a pretty tough philosophical question, and I thought we might discuss it."

Mike told him he was just finishing up making the family some homemade pizza and he'd have to call him back, but they agreed to Skype. When Mike got back to them and was introduced to Todd, Eric had Todd read the quote. He began but stopped after identifying the scientist who did the study. "I don't know…maybe the name of the anthropologist—Hrdy—is a typo or something," Todd said.

"Actually no," Mike said. "Hrdy is the way her husband's name is spelled. I think he has or had a medical practice out in Sacramento. It's an eastern European name—Czech, if I remember correctly."

Todd nodded. Then he read the quote through, finishing with, *"Do you still think God is good?"*

Mike took a moment to collect his thoughts. He was familiar with Williams' challenge. He'd dealt with it a few years earlier when he and a friend had done a study on the problem of evil.

"Just to be clear, Todd, Sarah Hrdy wasn't the one who asked the question; Dr. Williams was. And I think we can agree that his articulation of the infant monkeys' deaths was intended to be provocative. Why else would he have asked this? He's not stupid, though. He can't indict the langur for murder. Murder involves moral obligation, something no monkey has. So what's he doing?"

The two boys looked at each other. "He's making a case against God, for one," Todd then answered.

"Exactly,"[2] Mike replied. "He wonders how this kind of macabre situation can be reconciled with the idea of a God who is all-good and all-powerful. It's an absurdity to him. And if you allow him to suck you into this shell game of his, you'll miss the massive problem he's just created for himself."

Todd laughed. "He's just stuck it to God. How has he created a problem for himself?"

"Sticking it to God has and always will be one very good way to make problems for yourself," Mike answered dryly. "And I'll show you how that happened here, just from the standpoint of reason."

Seeing he had the boys' attention, Mike continued. "So here's the question, Todd. Where does Professor Williams get his idea of murder?"

"It's what happens when the lead ape is supplanted..."

"They're not apes; they're monkeys. And murder is precisely what's *not* going on in the harem, but we'll get to that," Mike said.

---

2   It should be noted that Williams did not consider himself an atheist, but he also clearly found the concept of a personal God expressed by the Judeo-Christian tradition untenable. The examples in nature he used in *The Pony Fish's Glow* showed this without question. On pages 152-153 he said, "Perhaps I should take a moment to deal with what I mean by *God*. I am not an atheist flaunting a caricature to offend people's religious sensitivities. In any theological discussion, I prefer to define atheism out of existence. Whatever entity or complex of entities is responsible for the universe being as we find it, rather than some other way or not there at all, can be called *God*." This would be the position of either a nominal deist or an agnostic. Yet, whatever his understanding of God, the example he chose, along with its attending question, was designed precisely to "flaunt a caricature." In his mind, our traditional view of God certainly needed to be readdressed. He was creating a picture to do just that.

"What I'd like to know, though, is where the concept of *murder* comes from. That's an idea Professor Williams knows about; that's part of his world but not part of theirs.

"You see, there is a moral threshold here. The ideas of *should* and *shouldn't* signify moral obligations. They are issues the professor had to deal with daily, but nowhere do monkeys have to deal with them. And that's the difference. So why would murder be a part of his knowing and not theirs? Where does the whole idea of moral obligations come from? Maybe Dr. Williams didn't realize it when he wrote this, but by raising the idea he brought the question back down on his own head."

Todd was quiet. He hadn't considered things from this angle.

Mike then observed, "There's a second issue here, and it has everything to do with his rhetorical strategy: the application of murder to the langur's actions—killing the infants when he takes over the harem. Williams was an evolutionary biologist—"

"Why are you now using the past tense with this guy?" Todd interrupted.

"He died in 2010."

Todd nodded his understanding, so Mike continued. "Williams, along with Peter Singer at Princeton, would be an example of, should I say, a militant or doctrinaire Darwinist. I'm not using these terms in a pejorative sense, mind you. People like this are just committed to applying evolution's implications consistently. Evolution understands mankind as simply an extension of the animal kingdom—we're not different in kind, only degree. So, for instance, if humans have rights, then animals have rights too. Peter Singer is a leading animal rights advocate."

"You disagree with animal rights?" Todd asked.

"No, only the basis of them," Mike replied. "Animal rights is a very Christian idea, actually. William Wilberforce, the English statesman who was instrumental in the abolition of slavery, was an animal rights advocate, but his rationale was decidedly different from Williams' or Singer's. To Wilberforce, mankind was truly different from the animal kingdom, not in degree but in kind. Man is made in God's image, but as such we don't *own* the world—we can't do with its creatures anything we like. We are, in fact, *stewards* of the world and, that being the case, have a responsibility to treat our fellow creatures humanely. The Bible speaks to the humane treatment of animals.[3] So in raising and harvesting animals for food or clothing, we need to be aware of their basic needs and welfare. And if we are going to kill them as part of that harvesting we don't do it brutally or callously; we do it humanely. God will hold us accountable. So conserving habitats for manatees and owls and protecting dolphins and sea turtles from the tuna nets are all very Judeo-Christian ideas.

"Where Williams got himself into trouble was when he conflated the idea of murder with the langur's actions.[4] He didn't mean to, but he brought up the other side of the coin. If humans are simply another animal, a mere extension of the animal kingdom, then why are we the only creature saddled with moral responsibility? Why aren't moral obligations or prohibitions part of the monkeys' picture as well?"

"I'm not following you," Todd admitted.

---

3   Deuteronomy 25:4, Proverbs 12:10.
4   Ironically, Williams concluded *The Pony Fish's Glow* by bemoaning the ease in which writers dealing with science employed "lubricious" slides by conflating terms and concepts in one domain (his four suggestions were material, moral, mental and codical) with those of another, contravening Hume's law – "…that moral directives cannot be deduced from descriptive premises." In other words, one cannot get an ought from an is. For whatever reason, he thoroughly violated his own prohibitions when handling Sarah Hrdy's research; langurs do not commit "murder."

"If we're not different in kind, only in degree," Mike continued, "and if humans have moral obligations and duties, then why don't they? Where does this moral threshold come from? Why don't we charge the cheetah with murder when it runs down the antelope and begins ripping it apart? Or the Orca when it terrorizes the poor seal before devouring it? If the Darwinists are taking their evolutionary worldview seriously, they have to admit, either the animals need to be held accountable for their actions, or we should no more be constrained by moral obligations than the langurs. Why are humans morally obligated while the rest of the animal kingdom gets off scot-free?"

Both boys were quiet and thinking. Then Todd shrugged and suggested, "Maybe our moral capacity is tied somehow to our advanced intellectual development. . .maybe."

Mike nodded quietly. "Well, let's think about that.

"At the end of World War II in Europe, the Western Allies— the United States and Britain—rushed in to capture the chief engineers of the Nazi war machine before the Russians could get to them. Why? Because we knew the Germans were two to three years ahead of us from the standpoint of technology. Swept-wing fighter-jet aircraft, ballistic and cruise missiles, superior battle-tank design. In this regard, the Nazis were way ahead. But morally they had degenerated to the monstrous. We found that out when we liberated the concentration camps. So I'm not sure the superior intellect idea flies."

Todd was stumped.

Mike then added, "What the Nazis show us is that the intellect is necessary but not sufficient."

"What's the difference?"

"Well," Mike responded thoughtfully, "fire needs oxygen to burn the forest down, so oxygen is necessary. But if it was also sufficient, every forest would automatically burn down in the presence of oxygen. That they don't shows it isn't. You need something more, something specific; a sufficient cause—a careless camper or a lightning strike."

Mike then continued quietly and deliberately, so both boys understood his questions were not simply rhetorical. "So. . .where *do* we come up with the concept of murder, and why should it matter? Professor Williams was disgusted enough about what went on in the monkey's harem to use it as an example, but why? Unless he believed he lived in a moral universe, he shouldn't have been. The fact is, he *did* believe in a moral universe; he couldn't have lived in a universe that wasn't. You'd have seen that side of him for sure if he'd caught one of his students cheating, or his stockbroker if the good professor had found out his managed funds were being embezzled.

"So here's the question: Do we, in fact, live in a moral universe? Do *objective* moral values exist—moral duties that are truly binding on all of humanity, in all human cultures, whether we believe them or not? Is the tin-horn dictator who reaches into his chemical stockpile and gases a village of civilians—men, women and children he feels pose a threat—a murderer, or was he just doing something politically or culturally unsavory? Was the holocaust a true evil or just something we believe was socially unacceptable—we'd have preferred it hadn't happened?"

Mike waited for a response, but there was none. "Let's be clear. In a Darwinian world, might makes right; the strong survive. So where does this concept of evil come from, the whole idea of the moral—shouldn't or ought?"

Mike grew quiet again to see if there was an answer forthcoming. "Todd...?"

Todd looked at Eric sheepishly and shrugged. Then he looked back at the screen so as to see Mike and admitted, "This is some good thinking. Is this why Eric's so straight-up when it comes to evolution? Because this sounds a lot like the way he makes sense of things."

Mike responded seriously, "Any great idea that makes great claims or has great consequences should be thoroughly cross-examined. Eric has learned to question his own faith in the same way."

The next day Mike got a call from Eric. "You handled that issue pretty well last night. We had a good chance to talk afterward. You really got him thinking."

Mike smiled. "He seems like a good guy, Eric. Tell me about him."

"He *is* a good guy," Eric said. "What you see is what you get; he's pretty comfortable in his own skin.

"He's a catcher for the team—a great ballplayer and a real leader. I got to know him when baseball camp started. I guess he found out I was a Christian, because he asked me early on if I believed when Jesus came back was I really going to meet Him in the air. I told him I did—that's what the Bible says[5]—so he calls me 'Fly-boy.'

5   1 Thessalonians 4:16-18; also see John 14:1-3 and 1 Corinthians 15:51, 52. (Note to the reader: None of these references speaks to Eric or Mike's belief about *when* Christ will return—at what point during what circumstances. It is simply an agreement with the Scriptures that Christ will gather His own to be with Him in a supernatural way.)

"From there, I guess he felt I'd be an easy mark. We're both biology majors. I am for premed, and he is for going into pharmaceutical research. He wants to own a research firm. Anyway, when the subject of evolution came up, he came after me pretty hard. But, thanks to you and Carl, I was able to turn things around quickly enough—stopped him in his tracks, actually—and I think I gained his respect. Plus he thinks I'm the best shortstop he's ever seen. . .high school or college anyway. Even though he's a sophomore, and I'm a lowly freshman, it was his idea that we be roommates.

"I don't suppose anyone outside of his immediate family other than me knows this—I asked him if I could share this with you and he said okay; you made a real impression on him last night—but when he was eight or nine, his family was going to a church that had altar boys, and he became one. It wasn't Roman Catholic. . .I'm not sure what it was. Anyway, one of the pastors was a pedophile and ended up molesting him for about six months."

"Aw, man!" Mike groaned angrily.

"Yeah. And being this authoritative, religious figure, the pastor somehow talked Todd into keeping it quiet. Well, when it came out, his dad went berserk. He had the pastor arrested—the guy's sitting in prison now. His dad also sued the church. . .or the denomination. Or both. I guess he got a settlement or something. Anyway, he was a stock broker or money trader of some kind—"

"Perhaps a currency trader," Mike interjected. "We have a couple of guys in my church who do that. If you know what you're doing, you can make a lot of money. If not, you'll lose your shirt."

"Well, his dad apparently knew what he was doing," Eric replied, "because he took the settlement and turned it into a big-time trust fund. Todd lacks for nothing. But then his dad owned a private plane and went on a hunting trip when Todd was, I think, thirteen, and the plane crashed, and his dad was killed. So Todd's got some deep-seated feelings about God, and they're not real positive."

"Yeah," Mike agreed soberly. "He's experienced some pain, that's for sure." Then he asked, "Have you shared with him what you went through last year?"

"Somewhat," Eric responded.

"So he knows you're not exempt from this sort of thing."

"He knows. He thinks it's pretty curious, or maybe even admirable, how Libby and I both handled things."

"And so you guys are good friends, eh?"

"Really good friends—probably lifetime," Eric said. "We trust each other…a lot of respect for each other—like you and Mr. Cohen." Ray Cohen had been both Libby—Eric's older sister— and his advanced biology teacher at Southside, the high school from which they'd each recently graduated. Ray and Mike had also worked together at the district level when Mike taught in another area high school.

Eric's comment reminded Mike of something. "I never told you about my meeting with Ray a few days after your state championship win last May, did I?"

"No. You met with Mr. Cohen?" Eric got a bit worried. "Did he figure us out?"

"Yepper," Mike answered. "Remember, he came up after the game? He came over to me after all the introductions had been made and, real quiet-like, let me know he wasn't at all keen about what you and I had pulled off in his class last year."

"Oh, man." Eric winced. "What did you do?"

"I agreed to meet with him the following week to sort through things; I'd been planning to anyway. We got together, and after I explained to him that keeping it from him was as much to protect him as anything he seemed to understand. I don't think he liked it much, but he was cool with it."

Then Mike added, "Did you know his eight-year-old daughter has cancer?"

"No!" Eric exclaimed.

"Yeah. It blew me away. Our girls are the same age and were at each other's first birthday parties. The condition is very serious—possibly fatal. It's called AML—Acute Myeloid Leukemia. Shands[6] is the hospital taking care of her. I've been in touch with Ray over the summer just to keep tabs on the situation. They've gotten close to some tipping-points where the condition might have gotten away from them, but they've all fought hard to keep her on the plus side. And it seems to be working.

"Poor guy," Mike added. "He was real candid about how all of this is beyond him—that he didn't have the tools to deal with it. I didn't know what to say. I just knew deep down that he wasn't going to find any real help outside of Christ, so I carefully suggested that he might consider trusting his Messiah about it. Jesus was his before he was mine."

"What did he say?"

"Thankfully, he didn't take offense. He initially gave me the standard Jewish reasons to dismiss Jesus—that he'd failed to bring in world peace or to conquer evil in any ultimate sense, which, in his mind, was what the Jewish Messiah was supposed

---

6   Shands is the teaching hospital associated with the medical school at the University of Florida, Gainesville.

to do. And a conversation began. When I opened up some of the Old Testament Scriptures to him,[7] he was exposed to a side of the argument he'd never considered. I guess he felt a little outflanked—the Scriptures aren't his forte—but it gave me a chance to make a great point about the whole debate surrounding what you and I had done."

"Tell me."

"His comment to me was, how was he supposed to know if I wasn't pulling something over on him? I knew more about the Jewish Scriptures than he did. So I told him I'd put him in touch with a counter missionary organization specifically designed to protect guys like him from guys like me—*Jews for Judaism*.[8] And they'd give him their rebuttal to everything I'd shared.

"He couldn't believe I'd do that, that I'd build this great case for Jesus being the Messiah then let someone undercut it, but I told him I had a couple of reasons. One, I didn't think for a moment that the God he and I worshipped—the God of the Christians and Jews—was in the least concerned about the truth being fully vetted; he'd want it that way. And two, the subject was important enough, and he was smart enough, to be exposed to both sides of the story. And hadn't Darwin said as much, 'A fair result can be obtained only by fully stating and balancing the facts and arguments on both sides of each question'?[9] I think he saw that our conversation had come full circle."

---

7 Genesis 49:10, Isaiah 53, Daniel 7:13, 14, Daniel 9:24-26, Micah 5:2, Zechariah 12:10.

8 www.jewsforjudaism.org. As an organization, this group is specifically designed to answer the issues raised by Jews for Jesus: www.jewsforjesus.org. To do what Darwin suggests, see the arguments from both sides and visit both websites.

9 Charles Darwin, *The Origin of Species*, sixth edition, Oxford, Oxford University Press, 1998, p. 4.

"Well, yeah!" Eric agreed.

"Anyway," Mike continued, "as we were leaving, he commented that conversations like we'd just had were not uncommon, and because of one a Jewish friend of his, who was a lawyer, had actually made a study of the trial of Jesus. And he pointed out some things about it that they found disturbing, things I hadn't recognized."

"Like what?"

"Well—let me see if I can remember this. For one thing, according to the *Mishnah*, a Jewish legal commentary dating from the third century AD, the trial of Jesus was marked by a number of very serious irregularities if not outright illegalities.

"Apparently the Sanhedrin, the Jewish Supreme Court that tried Jesus, was not supposed to meet at night.[10] They also weren't allowed to meet about a capital case, one with the possible outcome of a death sentence, on the eve of a Sabbath or major feast,[11] and they also weren't allowed to hand down a death sentence on the same day as a trial[12]—all of which happened in Jesus' case. Jesus, from the Gospel accounts, was physically abused during the proceedings, something also forbidden.

"But the other issue, to his lawyer friend, was that there was no *trial* really. Initially, the ruling body that had arrested Him was trying to get the charge of blasphemy to stick, and it wasn't turning out to be as easy as they'd thought. Then the high priest got impatient with the whole business, and he up and confronts Jesus about his claims, and Jesus affirms he's the Messiah. And bam! They've got

---

10 Mishnah, Sanhedrin, Chapter 4, Number 1.

11 Mishnah, Sanhedrin, Chapter 4, Number 1, and Mishnah, Betza, Chapter 5, Number 2.

12 Mishnah, Sanhedrin, Chapter 4, Number 1.

him. *And they went straight to the sentencing phase.* No investigation into whether Jesus could substantiate his claim—was he telling the truth, or was he a lunatic? Nothing. Ray said if it had been the latter—that Jesus was wacko—then it would have been at least a tragic miscarriage of justice. But if it was the former—that Jesus was who he claimed to be—then the consequences for the Jewish people would have been catastrophic. At that point he stopped and admitted that maybe that's what history has been saying. Maybe the Jewish leadership blew it two thousand years ago and missed their Messiah. But then Ray said something that showed me what a thinker he is."

"Tell me."

"He said, 'Maybe all this is true, and Jesus is the Messiah, and I should become a Christian, but what if that's not enough?'"

"Not enough?"

"Yeah," Mike continued. "He then launched into a very compelling litany about the problem of evil, all the human tragedy that surrounds us—famines, disease, the violence of nature and the miseries it causes. Then all the horror, death and destruction in the animal kingdom. So it's the same issue your roommate has thrown at you. Ray finished by saying, either God wants to do something about it but can't, or he can but doesn't want to. Either way it looked like a deal-breaker for him."

"What did you say?" Eric was mesmerized by the exchange.

"I told him there were answers to it, but until he made sense of Jesus they wouldn't make any sense to him. And he expressed an interest in discussing it further. In my now-and-then check-ins with him we talk a little bit. He's been pretty busy this summer taking care of his daughter and working on an advanced degree, but he's also been serious about his faith investigations. He's reading stuff from *Jews for Judaism* and from *Jews for Jesus*. He enjoys the fact that both sides of the debate are available to him. And I've given him some short pieces on the resurrection.[13] So it might be time to give him a call."

Mike got quiet for a moment, and an idea began to surface. "What if the four of us—you, Todd, Ray and I—got together at the Gator Skillet and did that breakfast club thing again?"

"Wow!" Eric lit up. "Would that be cool?!"

The summer between Eric's junior and senior years in high school, he'd met with Mike, along with the associate pastor at Mike's church, Carl Dunning. Eric's best friend in high school, Danny Miller, and Libby had also been participants. They met to discuss the many issues surrounding Darwinism and the Christian worldview. It had been a very heady experience, one he would always remember fondly. The idea that they might reconstitute anything like it was huge.

"Would Carl be able to join us? You two are a great team."

Mike answered, "Carl actually left this past June to take a church in Winston-Salem. He's always wanted to be the lead pastor in a church, and it looks like a great fit. He's very happy. I know he'd love to be back at the table with us, but the drive would be a killer."

Eric laughed at the obvious understatement, but then Mike added, "Seriously, though, Carl's going to be very interested in the

---

13   Mike had given Ray some introductory, summary writings on the subject, particularly Lee Strobel's coverage of the topic in *The Case for Christ,* with his interviews of Alexander Metherell, William Lane Craig, Gary Habermas and J. P. Moreland, and *The Case for the Real Jesus,* with his interview of Mike Licona. There is a whole world of scholarship on the historical case for Christ's bodily resurrection from the dead. See Gary Habermas and Mike Licona's *The Case for the Resurrection of Jesus* and N. T. Wright's *The Resurrection of the Son of God.*

fact that this subject has come up for you. The problem of evil, along with Darwinism, are the two subjects where the Christian community takes it in the teeth. You saw how deeply involved he is with evolution, and he's just as involved with this subject. I know he'd love to be here."

"You two keep in touch?"

"Yeah," Mike replied. "Today's technology allows us to. We text at least a couple of times a week."

Then something occurred to Eric, and he asked, "Could Libby join us? She'd be up for the discussion."

"It would be great to have her," Mike said. "And I'm sure Ray would love to see her again too."

Eric smiled to himself. "Yeah, so would Todd. Libby's caught his eye. He says she's *real* pretty, but even more, she's so mature—genuine, I guess, or transparent. . .unpretentious. But then she's religious. But is being religious what makes her prettier. . .or maybe more genuine. . . or just out of reach?"

By this time, Mike was laughing out loud.

Eric continued, "He's got all these little sorority babes and cheerleader types gushing over him, and he couldn't care less. Libby sees him as a nice guy—'really cute,' she says—but he's not on her radar. And he doesn't know what to do with that. Girls have never *not* been interested in Todd. But is he really interested in Libby? He doesn't know; he's just intrigued."

Mike tried to catch his breath. "Heck, that might be the ace in the hole."

"I don't know, Mike. Libby's got a list of things she's looking for, and it's pretty high and tight, and I don't think 'atheist' is on it. He'd have some real ground to make up, and he's pretty proud of being a free-thinker. She's not big on missionary dating either. Besides, even though she's nineteen, my sister is emotionally in her mid-twenties—you know that. Sophomore ballplayers are not going to get her attention."

Mike just laughed again. Everything Eric said was right on the money.

They both agreed to broach the idea to their respective contacts and then set things up. The breakfast club again—how cool was that?!

Chapter Two

No Apologies Necessary

Mike was the first to arrive at the restaurant that third Saturday in September, and he went straight back to the old, familiar booth. He was thankful it was empty.

"Mike!" Karen exclaimed. "What are you doing here?!"

Mike smiled brightly. "We were looking for the best waitress in Gainesville to take care of us, sweet and homey-like."

"You all coming back again?"

"Eric, Libby and I, for probably one or two meetings anyway. . .with a couple of new faces."

"I'm so glad! I'll do my best." Then she stopped herself and looked at him for a moment, a bit misty. "I miss my little buddy."

"We all do," Mike assured her.

"Well, you sit down *right here*," she said, pointing to the booth they'd used the year before, "and I'll get you some menus."

Eric, Libby and Todd were next on the scene. There were good, long hugs from Karen for the Jennings brother and sister and a kind welcome for Todd. Finally Ray arrived. He greeted Libby and Eric warmly, for which they were thankful—hugs, smiles and handshakes—as if nothing had happened.

They took a moment to get settled in, Todd and Ray being introduced to each other, and Karen sharing the daily specials. The regulars each had recommendations—their favorites on the menu—and the orders were taken quickly enough.

Once Karen was gone, Ray smiled and asked, "So this is where it all played out?"

"It wasn't personal, Mr. Cohen," Libby assured him quietly.

"I know," Ray replied. "Not any more than my handouts were that gave you so much trouble."

Todd spoke up. "I get the idea there's a significant history here that everyone's played a part in but me. Anybody want to clue me in?"

Everyone smiled knowingly. Then Ray shrugged. "I guess I was the one who precipitated that history, so maybe I ought to start.

"At the beginning of February a year ago Libby and Eric's dad was hurt working on a school at their mission station in the Dominican Republic. He fell off the roof and hurt his back pretty badly. The mission's home church is here in Gainesville, and with one of the best teaching hospitals in the country—Shands—they brought him back here to get him fixed up."

"And because I'd already been accepted into the premed program here at Florida," Libby added, "it was decided that it might be good for me to get some classroom experience and finish up my high school credits here. They also thought that because Eric's just a year behind me and following almost the exact same track he'd come too and maybe get to play some meaningful baseball."

Ray finished taking a sip of his coffee and then continued, "Anyway, Libby came into my class the last day of our unit on Darwin—a review day before the unit test. Since she'd been homeschooled for almost her entire academic career, she had a somewhat suspect understanding of the theory.

"I might also add, Todd, that whereas most teachers are satisfied that their students simply have a working knowledge of Darwinism, as someone who's believed it to be our best explanation of nature, and because it is the central dogma of modern biology, I've wanted my students to leave with a good bit deeper conviction about it, particularly if they are going to enter careers in science, be that research or teaching. So I've supplemented the regular textbook with handouts, examples given by some of America's premier Darwinists, as strong evidence for the theory. I didn't want my students just taking my word for it.

"Well, Libby took the handouts home, and her world began to come apart. . .in a big way."

Todd looked at Libby. "Why would that be?"

Libby smiled to herself, realizing how hard it was for someone not raised with the intense singularity of her faith to understand how corrosive something like Darwinism could be. She then asked the two men, "Who was it that said, 'Man is the result of a purposeless and natural process that did not have him in mind'?"[14]

---

14   George Gaylord Simpson, *The Meaning of Evolution*, revised edition, New Haven, CT, Yale University Press, 1967, p. 345.

"George Gaylord Simpson," Mike answered with an agreeing nod from Ray.

Libby then continued, speaking to Todd. "But my faith has taught me that God knows me, loves me and has a particular plan and purpose for my life. He loves and values this world, so I can love it and value it too. . .and sacrifice for it, when necessary. That's why I was going into medicine, to help the most vulnerable and needy—people, I believed, He loved and cared about.

"The handouts Ray gave me showed me a decidedly different picture of the world, one built by chance and therefore one with no ultimate meaning or value. The handouts—whale evolution, human/chimpanzee 'common descent' and other examples—were *very* compelling. I got a taste for the first time as to why institutional science sees Darwinism as the unquestioned explanation of nature and life as we know it. And it seemed I had good reason to doubt the Bible and to doubt all my faith had taught me. Going from living a life with immense purpose and value to one with neither was a very dark proposition, to say the least."

Ray immediately added, "And not an experience I want to repeat anytime soon. Libby's a class act, if you haven't noticed, Todd. And I hated seeing her go through that, but there was nothing I could do; she had to be prepared for the next level. What was your comment, Libby? 'If Darwinism is true then all I really am is sophisticated muck with a vivid imagination'?" He shook his head chuckling at the irony. "There's an idea for you—Libby Jennings as sophisticated muck. If it hadn't been for Sidney's comment—"

"What was that?" Libby asked.

"When you left that day, after you'd asked me how I squared Darwinism with being Jewish, I told Sid I was hoping you'd be okay. And she said, 'She will be. . .if God has anything to say about it.'"

"Sidney said that?" Libby asked, surprised at her classmate's insight. Sidney Duncan had been Libby's lab tablemate in advanced biology. She was the class wit, and, though she'd formed an immediate respect and affection for Libby, she wasn't particularly religious, at least not at that point.

Ray nodded. "Yeah, and oddly it was a comfort to me. I guess with the way things worked out, we might say she wasn't far off."

"So what's not personal?" Todd asked.

"Well, that was only the beginning of the story," Ray responded.

Eric now interjected, "Libby was going through hell, and watching her I wasn't far behind. Nor were Mom and Dad. They didn't know what to do.

"Danny, my best friend, had the same thing happen to his brother, who was going to the University of Michigan. His brother lost his faith going through something almost identical, though, unlike Libby, he apparently didn't mind. So Danny could relate to my heartache. Losing his brother in the same way, he had his own pain. He was a real comfort."

Then a quizzical look came across Eric's face. "What is it with me and catchers, anyway? Two of my best friends over the past three years—you and Danny—have been catchers."

"We can't help it," Todd replied. "We're just trying to survive being on the receiving end of that amazing playmaking of yours, wondering where in your next 'Derek Jeter' move that ball's going to come at us—from what insane angle and at what speed."

Ray nodded. "I saw Eric at the state championship game in May, and I thought he was good." Looking at both Mike and Todd, he asked, "But you baseball types think Eric's that special?"

Mike nodded while Todd remarked, "He's *that* special."

Eric smiled appreciatively. Then he continued, "But Danny had no answers. Anyway, we were getting geared up for the district playoffs, and Mike showed up at practice one day as the local Athletes for Christ area rep. Coach Washington introduced us, and in talking after practice I found out that Mike was a former high school science teacher. So I shared my angst about my sister's situation and then started grilling him about evolution. He gave me some really good historical background, and it sounded like he knew what he was talking about."

"He normally does," Ray said, affirming his friend.

"Anyway," Eric continued, "we finished up by talking about what to do for Libby. Interestingly, Mike also knew Mr. Cohen—I mean...." Looking at Ray, he asked, "Do we call you Ray now?"

Ray nodded with a smile.

Eric thought that was cool and smiled too. "Anyway, Mike knew Ray and showed he had a lot of respect for him, so I knew it wasn't going to be a personal thing, where you just slam the other side; it was going to be about the science. Mike said to help Libby he'd need to see the handouts, and then maybe we could set up a study group over the summer and look at them from another direction and include her."

"This is like a movie," Todd smiled as he tried to take it all in. "So Libby lets you see the handouts, Mike?"

"Not initially," Eric answered for him. Then to Ray, he said, "She wasn't going to put you in any kind of position where you could be publicly criticized."

Ray smiled at Libby, appreciating her loyalty.

Libby then added, "I didn't know who Mike was or what he'd do with them. Then I met him at the district championship game, and he turned out to be everything Eric had said he was—a straight up guy." Looking at Mike fondly, she said, "So after Eric put his really smelly uniform in the trunk of my car, I gave Mike the handouts, and we must have spent—what—an hour and a half in the bleachers after that game talking about them?" Mike nodded.

"Okay, boys and girls," Karen interrupted, followed by an assistant server with three trays full of food.

After the various orders got to their respective places, Todd looked at Mike. "So you were familiar with all the info on those handouts?"

"Yeah," Mike said, thoughtfully. "The associate pastor at my church and I shared duties teaching an adult Sunday school class called 'Darwinism and Design.' And we'd taught from just about every example Ray'd given his class in those handouts."

"So he was able to answer all your questions?" Todd asked Libby. "And you were able to go back to your faith as you knew it, I take it?"

Libby nodded, so Todd said to the two men, "I think it's remarkable that you two guys who view this stuff so differently are sitting at the same table eating breakfast together. You must really respect each other...or like each other...or both."

Mike and Ray looked at one another then nodded and answered, "Both," together.

"But I still don't see where this apology that's apparently 'not necessary' is…not needed," Todd said.

"Originally," Mike said, "the study group idea was to prepare Eric for the information in the handouts, so he could go through Ray's class without experiencing the kind of tailspin his older sister had. It was also supposed to be a neutral learning environment for Libby, to give her the other side to the picture she'd gotten in Ray's class. That was the plan anyway, but then she and I ended up doing all of that in that conversation after the game."

Then, gathering his thoughts, he continued, "But it was an observation she made that got me rethinking what the summer study might become. One of the handouts Ray had given her was by a professor at Brown University, Kenneth Miller, and his supposed debunking[15] of an intelligent design proponent— Michael Behe's—argument on the 'irreducible complexity'[16] of the cilium.[17] But I couldn't find anything in the handouts from Behe, only Miller. And that was frustrating. I'd have thought, just to be fair, Ray should have included Behe's original argument in his own words. He was the guy who originated the argument about cilia. And I speculated that perhaps Ray hadn't done that because it doesn't take much to get a teacher in trouble when dealing with this material. And letting an intelligent design guy speak for himself was one of those things."

"I don't follow you," Todd said.

15 Kenneth Miller, *Finding Darwin's God*: A Scientist's Search for Common Ground between God and Evolution, New York, NY, HarperCollins, 1999, pp. 140-143.

16 For a discussion on irreducible complexity, see Appendix I – Exposing a Darwinian Straw Man.

17 Michael Behe, *Darwin's Black Box, The Biochemical Challenge to Evolution,* New York, NY, Touchstone-Simon & Schuster Inc., 1998, pp. 59-73.

"When I was a teacher," Mike continued, "I knew I was skating on thin ice when I questioned Darwinism's purely materialistic explanation for life, its origin and development. You can't do that in public education. Simply by raising the question, I was exposing myself to the possibility of being charged with violating the 'separation of church and state'—supposedly for trying to introduce my 'religious sentiments' into the classroom."

"How's that?" Todd replied.

Mike smiled thoughtfully. "Well, questioning one is tantamount to proposing the other in our current educational and legal environment. The National Center for Science Education[18] and their buddies over at the ACLU[19] can get real excited real quick and start making noise about creating a protracted legal fight the local school board can't afford, and then I'm down at the district office in a meeting with the superintendent and his legal team. Anyway, not knowing why Ray hadn't included Behe, I suggested to Libby that we give him the benefit of the doubt." Looking back to Ray, Mike asked, "Was I right?"

Ray shook his head no. "It was just an oversight on my part. Kenneth Miller's my guy, or was, and I just felt his take on Behe was fair and complete enough, and I didn't want to load the students up with a duplication of the same argument. So I was just letting Miller speak for Behe. That was a mistake."

"Why?" Todd asked.

---

18 The National Center for Science Education is an organization formed to defend Darwinism's sole and privileged position in public science education. Along with the ACLU, they are involved at the legal level virtually anywhere Darwinism is challenged in public school education.

19 American Civil Liberties Union.

"Because Miller botched it," Ray answered. "I didn't realize it until Eric began questioning the handout in class, but Behe made one case and Miller answered another. Some call it a 'straw man'[20] argument, and in this instance it's a fair criticism."

Libby then interjected, "And that's exactly what Mike pointed out to me. But in our trying to defend Ray I was introduced to this insane idea that, in public education, a teacher can't legally discuss the pros *and* cons of evolution. And it occurred to me that maybe they could come after the teacher if he questions evolution, but what about the student? Could Eric or I raise a question in class without creating some kind of legal quagmire?"

"And a big, thousand-watt light bulb went off in my head," Mike laughed as he mentally replayed the conversation.

Todd nodded. "Oh, I get it now. You not only gave Eric your side of the story about the handouts, but you also trained him to go into your friend's classroom and question the theory?"

Mike and Eric nodded.

"This is amazing!" Todd exclaimed. And then looking at Ray, he asked, "But you're saying an apology isn't necessary? Why the heck not??! He sent a prepped student into your classroom to subvert what you were teaching. I'd have been livid."

"Well, I wasn't happy about it when I finally figured it out," Ray admitted. "But I knew Mike. He was a guy I'd grown to trust. Our daughters were at each other's first birthday parties. We'd worked together. Sure, I was miffed, but I tried to keep the lid on it, to keep myself emotionally in check until we talked. Besides, what Eric did, in the way he did it, did nothing to compromise my leadership or embarrass me. It actually made the class a lot more interesting."

20   See Appendix I – Exposing a Darwinian Straw Man.

"Unbelievable...." Todd was incredulous.

"Not really," Ray replied. "As a teacher, I do my best to make the classroom experience as interactive and engaging as I can. My students learn better that way. The way Eric went about it, it quietly opened up the subject. And really, if you think about it, every question he raised gave me a better opportunity to make the case *for* Darwinism."

"This is crazy." Todd shook his head.

Ray shrugged, "Well, again not as crazy as you might think. Mike's absolutely right, Todd. If a teacher questions Darwin, he's opening him or herself up to possible litigation. So, for all intents and purposes, the theory is absolutely protected from any kind of balanced scrutiny."

Mike then clarified, "So my purpose in keeping Ray in the dark was two-fold. Ray is known as one of the best science teachers in the district, not only because of his grasp of the subject, which is considerable, but in the way he teaches. He has absolute command of the classroom. His students love him, and he makes them want to work. So, if this idea was going to fly, I figured, if it could be pulled off in Ray's class, it could be done anywhere. But, second, it needed to be done in a way that protected him from becoming any kind of accessory."

Todd looked at Ray in bemused bewilderment. "So how did you finally catch onto this?"

Ray replied, "It took a while." To clarify things, he added, "It didn't occur to me this kind of thing would go on or that a guy like Eric—Mr. Joe-Christian-Missionary-Guy—would do something so sneaky, so shrewd."

Everyone laughed.

"But then we got to whale evolution," Ray continued, "and his questioning was simply too good. I figured at that time he was being or had been coached. It was only later that I found out who the coach was."

Todd laughed at what he perceived as an absurd situation. "Coached or not, we *know* whales evolved." He looked at Ray but was not getting the assurance he'd expected. "You still believe that the whales evolved, right?"

Ray quietly shook his head. "Eric's questions were a deal-breaker. Whale evolution will forever lack the punch it used to. In fact, post-Eric, most of those handouts are being rethought."

"You're kidding, right?" Todd said. "I mean, what's the big argument? From what I can tell, whale evolution is a done-deal in Darwinism. If he's got an argument that takes out that idea, I'd like to know about it."

"You can ask Eric about that later," Mike replied. He didn't want this morning's discussion to go too far afield. "Darwinism can and will be an ongoing discussion for all of us for a long time to come, but not now. Now we need to address the subject I wanted to get us together for, and that's the problem of evil. Ray had brought this up in a conversation he and I were having in May, so after we'd" —at this Mike pointed to both young men— "Skyped the other day, I called Ray and asked him to put together his thoughts in a couple of questions we could discuss."

Todd couldn't believe they were leaving the whale topic so unresolved, but everyone else seemed to be good with it. Apparently they were all well-versed in the argument and wanted to move on.

At this, Ray opened a file folder he'd brought with him and handed everyone a page with two questions on it. The first one read:

1) Why in a universe created wholly by an omniscient, omnipotent and omni-benevolent God is evil a component at all?

Ray commented, "This first question is based on the notion of cause and effect. And it's pretty simple really. If God is the sole source of creation, the sole source of this effect we call our existence, then *everything* in the effect must be attributable to the cause."

"Why's that?" Eric inquired.

"Because, if it can't be," Ray said, "then the effect in question—evil—must have arisen from some other source. Nothing comes from nothing. So are we positing something other than God as the source of anything here?"

Eric shook his head no.

"We either have to be able to attribute evil to God, or God—the great uncaused Cause—is not the only necessary Being out there. Something else is messing with this creation, or there's another answer."

"And constructing a theodicy,"[21] Mike added, "is about that very thing. Christian theism accepts the premise that God is the only necessary Being and the sole source of creation, but it answers evil's existence in other ways."

"Which will prove interesting, I'm sure." Ray chuckled. "We'll see if the answers Mike has for us are valid or just a song and dance."

Mike nodded and smiled assuredly that he was up to the challenge.

---

21   The term theodicy is a combination of two Greek words, *Theos*, meaning God, and *dike*, meaning justice. The purpose of a theodicy is to explain how the existence of evil can be reconciled with the existence of a holy, righteous and loving God without holding God in any way culpable for the phenomenon.

Ray then read the second question:

2) How can an all-powerful, all-loving God seemingly sit so idly by as evil and suffering ravage what He has made?

He added, "And this, I think, is the harder of the two questions. It's certainly the one on the minds and lips of my friends, both secular and religious."

"But before we get going," Mike said, "I want to make something clear: Evil can be an event—something we, or whoever, might *experience*—or it can be a theoretical problem— *a topic* of study. And they're two very different things.

"For someone to try to give a rationale to Ray that his daughter is sick because he's in some way morally deficient, or that your dad did something bad, Todd, and that's why his plane crashed, would be to *add to* the suffering—actually to increase the evil. God doesn't seem to take kindly to that sort of thing, and all one has to do is read the book of Job to see God's attitude toward Job's philosophizing 'friends.' Paul is clear that, for the Christian, there is no place for this kind of thing. Instead, we are simply to rejoice with those who rejoice and mourn with those who mourn.[22] So our meeting to discuss the problem of evil is not to dissect any specific event or experience or the role God might have played in it or his rationales, but to discuss the broad *subject*. We're going to take a reasoned approach to the problem of evil as a philosophical and theological challenge. There's no place for any speculation as to why a typhoon struck the Philippines or a tornado hit Moore, Oklahoma. That's

---

22   Romans 12:15.

simply unbridled speculation with no conceivable basis and so is out of bounds. Agreed?"

All nodded that they were on board.

Chapter Three

Inescapable

"So," Mike offered, "I'm going to suggest that the rest of our time together this morning be spent dealing with Ray's first question. The two he's articulated are profound because they speak to two answers a theodicy attempts to give: one is to evil's origin, and the other is to its purpose."

"You used that term a minute ago," Ray observed. "Just what is a *theodicy?*"

Mike apologized. "I'm getting ahead of myself. In Christian theology or philosophy, a theodicy is not just a defense that shows attacks on God because of evil's existence are inadequate; it's a positive argument that attempts to answer one or both of these questions and do so without holding God culpable. The term was first coined by a pre-Enlightenment mathematician and philosopher named Gottfried Leibniz.[23]

"Most Christians will start with some basic assumptions," he continued. "One of those is that God is absolutely holy. This means he is the embodiment of moral perfection and, as such, cannot be the originator of evil in any volitional way."

"Meaning…?" Todd asked.

"Though God might have known evil was inevitable, he didn't think it up, did not choose it or create it, and does not perpetrate it."

"That's not what the Old Testament says." Ray chuckled. "Knowing we were going to discuss this this morning, I did a little research of my own." He found a note he'd written himself on his smart phone and read: "I form the light, and create darkness: I make peace, and create evil: I the Lord do all these things."[24]

Todd laughed. "Wow! Where do you go with that, Mike? I mean, how much clearer can the indictment be? This is as self-incriminating as God can get, don't you think?"

"Actually no, Todd," Mike responded calmly. "The reference to evil in this passage can be, and most often is, translated as 'calamity,' the tools of God's judgment or correction. But it doesn't speak of *moral* evil—any type of falsehood or betraying the truth—so it doesn't implicate Him in that."

"Does that calamity result in death or dismemberment or suffering?" Todd followed up.

"Undoubtedly."

"Well, then," he replied, "shouldn't God be held accountable for the death and misery he causes?"

---

23   Gottfried Leibniz (1646-1716) was German and is characterized in some philosophical circles as the last "universal genius."

24   Isaiah 45:7, KJV/Cambridge Ed (see also Lamentations 3:37, 38 and Amos 3:6).

Mike asked, "So let me get this straight: the court that sentences the child rapist and killer to death, resulting in his incarceration, isolation, misery and the eventual ending of his life, should somehow be held accountable for the ultimate '*murder*' of the rapist?"

Todd's facial expression was initially skeptical but then changed as Mike's point sank in.

"In defense of Todd's position, Mike," Ray interjected, "you'd have to admit lots of innocent people get caught in the crossfire when these calamities or judgments occur."

"And there are two answers for that," Mike told Ray. "We'll get to those. One issue immediately cited by theologians and philosophers is whether or not any of us are really 'innocent.'"

Ray's face showed a quiet disapproval. "I'm not sure that citation is valid; we might have to come back to that."

Mike showed he understood the objection, so Ray nodded that he'd give Mike the time and, for now, the leeway to make a case. Ray then continued, "So we're back to the cause and effect question: How is God the sole source of this universe, and yet evil is such a prevalent characteristic…or a characteristic at all?"

"And answering that without implicating God *is* the trick," Mike replied. "The first tack Christian thinkers have taken is to determine what evil *is*. Is evil a thing—something requiring a godlike being to conceive of or create it—or is it the *antithesis* of 'thingness'?"

"You're losing me quickly, Mike," Ray said, with a nod of agreement from Todd.

Mike understood completely; he'd been in both of their shoes at one time. "The early Christian theologian, Augustine of Hippo,[25]

---

25 Augustine (354-430) was bishop of Hippo in North Africa from 395 until his death in 430. He is considered one of the greatest of early Christian thinkers. He

raised this question," he continued. "Is evil something in and of itself, or is it simply the corruption of something else, something that does exist in and of itself? If it's the former, if it has its own substantial nature like that of good, then on what basis do we choose one over the other? They're ontological equals.[26] C. S. Lewis, a renowned Christian scholar, raised this question using the figures of good and evil in Zoroastrian dualism,[27] where they *are* viewed as ontological equals and the struggle an eternal one." Mike brought up the quote on his tablet and read:

The metaphysical difficulty is this: the two Powers, the good and the evil, do not explain each other. Neither Ormuzd (the personification of good) nor Ahriman (the personification of evil) can claim to be the Ultimate. More ultimate than either of them is the inexplicable fact of their being there together. Neither of them chose this tête-à-tête. Each of them, therefore, is *conditioned*—finds himself willy-nilly in a situation; and either that situation itself, or some unknown force which produced that situation, is the real Ultimate. Dualism has not yet reached the ground of being. You cannot accept two conditioned and mutually independent beings as the self-grounded, self-comprehending Absolute. On the level of picture-thinking this difficulty is symbolized by our inability to think of Ormuzd and Ahriman without smuggling in the idea of

is claimed by all branches of Christianity—Roman Catholic, Eastern Orthodox and Protestant.

26   Ontological is the understanding of something's essence—its essential nature. If both good and evil have equal substance or essence, choosing between them becomes problematic, as C. S. Lewis explains.

27   Dualism is the juxtaposition of opposites—good and evil, light and dark.

a common *space* in which they can be together and thus confessing that we are not yet dealing with the source of the universe but only with two members contained in it. Dualism is a truncated metaphysic.

The moral difficulty is that Dualism gives evil a positive, substantive, self-consistent nature, like that of good. If this were true, if Ahriman existed in his own right no less than Ormuzd, what could we mean by calling Ormuzd good except that we happened to prefer *him?* In what sense can the one party be said to be right and the other wrong? If evil has the same kind of reality as good, the same autonomy and completeness, our allegiance to good becomes the arbitrarily chosen loyalty of a partisan. A sound theory of value demands something different. It demands that good should be original and evil a mere perversion; that good should be the tree and evil the ivy; that good should be able to see all round evil (as when sane men understand lunacy) while evil cannot retaliate in kind; that good should be able to exist on its own while evil requires the good on which it is parasitic in order to continue its parasitic existence.[28]

Mike summarized, "Viewing evil as *something*, rather than merely the corruption of something, is problematic."

"I'm still back here in the dust, Mike," Todd said.

"For rust to occur, Todd, the steel must first exist. Rust cannot exist on its own; it's the corruption of the steel. For there to be

---

28 C. S. Lewis, *God in the Dock*, Grand Rapids, MI, William B. Eerdmans Publishing Co., 1973, pp. 22, 23 (parentheses mine).
GOD IN THE DOCK by C.S. Lewis copyright© C.S. Lewis Pte. Ltd. 1970. Extract reprinted by permission.

a hole in the cloth, the cloth must first exist; the hole can only be where something else was. As a moral example, adultery can only take place if a marriage exists. One is primary and substantial; its own corruption is dependent on that. Evil's existence is then dependent on the existence of the good it becomes the corruption of. This understanding is what has given Christian thinkers the idea that evil is a contingent phenomenon and not something that possesses ontological or existential equality. And what this gave Augustine the opportunity to do was recognize evil as an uncreated non-substance having no beginning and therefore no cause *or* creator. So, in his mind, the case against God as the originator of evil was dismissed."

Ray smiled broadly. "Now if that isn't an example of some slick thinking, I don't know what is." He shook his head. "I think he scored some points; I can follow the distinctions he made—bright guy, this Augustine fellow—but the same basic problem remains. Whether evil is something or not—a *non*-something, I guess—it's a prevalent *characteristic* of our existence and must be accounted for. Why can steel rust? Why should corruption occur at all?"

Libby and Eric were quiet, believing Mike was up to the task, but Todd thought Ray had scored some points.

"Ray's right," Todd said. "This whole deal is God's. All of this has happened on his watch. Who is ultimately responsible if not him? He can do anything, right?"

Libby and Eric looked at each other smiling, knowing exactly what was coming next.

"God can do *anything*?" Mike asked.

"Sure; he's omniPOtent." Todd laughed at his own mispronunciation.

Mike smiled. "Can he make a married bachelor?"

"What…? Is this a trick question?"

"You said he could do anything."

Todd shook his head no.

"Can he make a three-sided square?"

Todd thought for a moment. "No."

Mike asked one more. "Did God choose to exist?"

Todd smiled. "He'd have to exist to choose to do anything including existing, so I guess not."

"Things either exist necessarily, or they are the consequence of something that does; they're contingent. Why? Because, like Ray said, nothing comes from nothing; there is no third option. In logic, this is called the Law of the Excluded Middle. God either exists necessarily, making him a necessary Being, or he was created…by a necessary Being.[29] So, Todd, if you're looking for something an 'omniPOtent,' eternal Someone can't do, you've found it; he cannot *not* exist."

Mike shrugged. "There are, in fact, lots of things God can't do. He can't create a rock so big he can't pick it up anymore than we can taste a number. In other words, he can't do the absurd—the logically incoherent or inconsistent. He can only do what can be done. He is limited by the fundamental nature of reality—its structure."

"So did reality exist first?" Ray asked.

"Nothing exists if God doesn't exist," Mike replied. "God *is* reality, the basis for anything and everything else. Your rabbis would agree. Reality is simply an extension of his existing…and his nature."

"Including the reality of evil?" Ray smiled.

---

29   This is the basis for the answer to the question: Why is there something instead of nothing?

"We'll get there," Mike assured him as he began searching for something else on his tablet. "I want to read one more thing to you, something from a Catholic scholar named Jacques Maritain, a French philosopher, from a series of talks he gave at Marquette University back in the early forties, in which he dealt with this very thing.

Suppose we take a craftsman who must cut wood in a straight line according to a ruler; if he does not cut it in a straight line, that is, if he makes a bad cutting, that bad cutting will be caused by the fact that the craftsman did not hold the ruler in his hand. Similarly, delectation (pleasure, enjoyment) and everything that happens in human affairs should be measured and ruled according to the rule of reason and divine law…. And for that very absence or that lack which consists in not making use of the rule, not taking the rule in hand, *there is no need to seek a cause, for the very freedom of will, whereby it can act or not act, is enough…*

Evil lies in acting without reference to the rule; and in this concrete whole, acting without consideration of the rule, there are two moments to be distinguished, not with regard to time but according to ontological order; *first moment, not considering the rule,* which is a negation, an absence, the lack of a good which is not yet due; and *second moment, acting with that negation,* which, from the sole fact that one acts with it, becomes a privation, an absence of a due good in the action…. [The creature] has put an absence at the head of its acting, it has introduced the condition which will cause the texture of being to give way…. We must therefore necessarily have recourse to a paradoxical language and say the created will then "does nothingness," "it makes non-being."[30]

"What Maritain is describing here, where the created *will* 'does nothingness,' 'it makes non-being' is the uncaused nature of evil; that at its origination it can only be attributed to the will—it 'lies in *acting* without reference to the rule,' and what results."

Ray nodded, as if he was beginning to put a picture together. "The French philosopher does a good job, and I think I'm following him. But do you have a real world example we can hang his conceptual pieces on?"

Mike grew thoughtful. "Okay, let's say Phil dearly loves his wife, Mary; they've got a great marriage. But then Mary is involved in a car accident which leaves her severely disabled—paralyzed, brain damage, the whole tragic picture. Phil is devoted to his wife, but after a year or so of taking care of her, he's tired and lonely. Yet all he can see lying ahead of him are years of simply taking care of and supporting an invalid. She can no longer serve the role of a wife—a companion or a lover. He knows he made a vow to her to be faithful for richer, for poorer, in sickness and in health, as long as they both lived, but golly…!

"He then runs into Susan, a colleague from work, while at the gym. She is very single, very attractive and very sympathetic. You can see where I'm going. When he considers another relationship, meaning the fundamental violation of his wedding vows, he's involved in Maritain's 'negation.' When he enters into a sexual

---

30   Maritain, Jacques, *St. Thomas and the Problem of Evil,* Milwaukee, WI, Marquette University Press, 1942, pp. 25, 31, 33, 34 (parentheses mine).

relationship with this other woman, it becomes privation—the destruction of his marriage."

"Come on, Mike," Todd said, as a serious appeal. "I have no interest in being a cad here, but can you blame him? What good does it do to try to remain faithful to vows that certainly one of them no longer remembers or can probably even understand and imprisons the other to a life of married singleness?"

Libby sensed Todd's sincerity—they all did—but something more important was at stake. "So why did he make the vows in the first place?"

"He was in love," Todd answered seriously. "He meant them. He would have worked to make the marriage a lifetime commitment. But this isn't a marriage anymore."

"So do the vows mean nothing?" Eric asked.

Todd shook his head in exasperation. "And this is why I don't like the whole concept of moral absolutes. It gives us no room to maneuver. We're not free to apply *humane* solutions to situations like this. And those of us who want to end up being seen as somehow morally suspect...!"

"The humane solution, Todd, is why I'm not a moral relativist," Mike replied. "The vows are placed there precisely to protect someone like Mary from being abandoned at the point when she's most vulnerable. She can do nothing to protect herself or provide for herself. She was depending on the love and commitment of her husband to do that.

"The second reason for the vows is to move the focus from the individual to the family. God knows that as the family goes, so goes the society and culture. If the wishes and fulfillment of the individual are placed above protecting the integrity of the family, all is lost. The family, not the individual, is the basic building block of any society, like the cell is in the body."

"Why's that?" Todd challenged. "Why *not* the individual?"

"Because the individual can't reproduce," Mike answered. "It can't create a next generation; it can't perpetuate the culture. At the biological level, the cell is the smallest reproducing entity in the body. If the integrity of the cell is compromised—if a cell becomes cancerous—and it goes unchecked, it will kill the body. In the same way, if the structure of the family is allowed to be eroded, the culture disintegrates. Welcome to America in the twenty-first century. Today only twenty percent of all households are married couples with children—the traditional nuclear family.[31] Here and now the human fulfillment of the individual is king, and we, as a nation, are reaping the consequences. American culture is coming apart at the seams."[32]

Todd just got quiet.

---

31   Huffington Post, January 25, 2013, *The Disappearing Nuclear Family and the Shift to Non-Traditional Households Has Serious Financial Implications for Growing Numbers of Americans.* To clarify, less than forty-eight percent of households in America are made up of married couples—young marrieds yet to have children or couples who can't or have chosen not to have children, empty-nesters and retirees. The majority are single individuals, or single-parent families, for whatever reason, couples cohabitating or non-traditional homosexual and lesbian households. The trend should be very disturbing for the future of our society.

32   Every alternative to a lifelong monogamous, heterosexual marriage (fornication, adultery, incest, bestiality and homosexuality) was firmly condemned in the Mosaic Law. The surrounding cultures, particularly those inhabiting Canaan (Palestine) prior to the Jews conquering the land, believed and practiced institutional adultery— cult prostitution and fertility rites—along with bestiality, etc., all of which allowed husbands (and wives) to find sexual expression and satisfaction outside the bonds of marriage and the family. It was highly destructive to the family unit and the culture in general and was therefore a capital crime under Old Testament law. (For an excellent treatment of this subject, see *Is God a Moral Monster?*, Paul Copan, pp. 107-109: No Female Priests?)

Libby's phone vibrated, showing she was receiving a text. She looked down to read it then told Mike as an aside, "Chelsea will be here in a few minutes."

"Please tell her to come in," Mike said.

When Mike looked back at Todd, Ray said, "It still doesn't add up, Mike. Sin, as you call it, or evil or privation, can't all be laid upon our free will. There are lots of free choices I can make that have no moral ramifications. I can choose waffles or pancakes or bacon and eggs here. I can go to the grocery store and choose wheat or white, crunchy or creamy, chocolate chip or rocky road. None of these choices is bad; they have no moral implications whatsoever. There's got to be a missing piece here. So what is it?"

Mike nodded his understanding. "When Carl and I were studying this together, we ended up with the same sense about the missing piece you have." He went on. "For evil to be chosen, it must first become a choice. And that piece involves an element in Maritain's lectures he assumed and therefore never overtly developed: the *indispensable* role of the straightedge itself."

"Indispensable?" Todd queried. "What's so indispensable about the straightedge? You don't need a ruler to draw a straight line."

The four others looked at him knowing he wanted to make a point. "Really?" Libby asked.

"Watch," he said. Taking a flyer from the shelf behind them, he drew a very straight-ish line between three and four inches long freehand.

Libby challenged him. "That's not a line; that's a dash—a hyphen." Picking up another of the flyers, she turned it over to the blank side and put one finger on the upper left-hand corner and another on the bottom right-hand corner. "Now draw a line this long."

Todd smiled at her astute challenge and then did his best. Remembering a tactic her dad had used countless times to determine the usability of a two-by-four, Libby picked up the paper and held it nearly edge on. This compressed the image of the line so she could more easily see how well or badly he'd done. "Not too straight, Todd." She shook her head in a friendly disapproval.

Todd shrugged a laugh. "It's as straight as I can make it."

Eric picked up the paper and did the same thing. "Well... does that mean it's as *absolutely* straight as it can be, or is it mildly crooked?"

"It's mildly straight." Todd smiled at his own play on Eric's words.

The true implications of Maritain's point now having dawned on him, Ray said flatly, *"It's crooked."* All three teens were struck by his emphatic tone, and they stayed quiet waiting to see where he'd go with this. Ray looked at Mike, and his eyes narrowed. Then he added to the teens, "Without the straightedge, neither concept—straight or crooked—exists. The straightedge is what makes either possible; it provides the basis for them to mean anything at all."

"You need the ruler to do all that?" Todd asked incredulously.

"Maritain uses a ruler or straightedge," Mike said, "because he's talking about a woodcutter. But the example can be a plumb line or a chalk line or anything else, anything that allows for the standard to be *objectively* established and therefore a way to identify both the rule and its exception or violation. You see, Todd, it's the mere existence of the standard or value, *any* standard or value, that automatically and inescapably creates the potential for its own violation; otherwise the violation itself is impossible."

Todd lifted his hands and shrugged that the point was still not clear, so Mike continued, "Can you steal something not owned, that doesn't *belong* to anybody?"

Todd took a moment to think about the question, then chuckled. "No." He wasn't stupid.

"Can you run a stop sign that doesn't exist or exceed a speed limit not posted?"

Todd kept smiling at the utter simplicity of the questions and shook his head no.

"The law—the speed limit sign—tells you both what's legal and therefore, by consequence, what's not," Mike clarified. "So when is the fundamental potential for adultery created?"

Todd shook his head; he was ready for someone else to be the object of the questions. Then Ray answered for them both. "When Isaac and Rebecca say, 'I do.' Like you said, Mike, it's an inescapable part of the package."

Mike smiled at Ray's use of good biblical names for the example and added. "Before their wedding, adultery is not possible. The potential for faith-*less*-ness can only be born when a commitment to faith-*ful*-ness is made…just like the potential for theft is created by ownership or law-breaking is created by the laws themselves. Again, *it's the mere existence of the standard or value, any standard or value, that automatically and inescapably creates the potential for its own violation."*

"So the takeaway is, as you said, Mike, God did not create it or choose it. Like the straightedge creates the possibility for the crooked," Ray said, nodding as the conclusion became apparent, "evil's *potential* is a fundamental and inescapable result of his *holy* existence."

Mike smiled with satisfaction; his friend was getting the picture.

"So," Ray now summarized, "we might say that evil is as much evidence for God's existence as good is."

"Good in the objective, moral sense, along with *true* evil, would be impossible otherwise," Mike replied.

"Wow...I didn't see that coming," Ray said, shaking his head quietly.

Mike said, "That's why the concept of objective moral values is a category inaccessible to atheism. To even mention the idea of *real* evil is an admission of a *holy* God's existence. Atheists can be very moral; the ones I know are. They just have no objective basis to work from."

Things got quiet for a moment. Then Libby asked, "So have we answered your first question, Ray?"

Ray nodded thoughtfully. "Yes, we have." Then he added, "So I guess it's the *perpetuation* part of the issue that's still hanging out there. How is it that God sees all of this garbage going on—all the pain and suffering and mayhem—and supposedly has the power to do something about it but seemingly does nothing?"

"And getting into that would take us past lunch." Mike smiled. "And I have tickets to the Gator game this afternoon and need to get ready."

Libby spied her friend trying to find her in the crowded restaurant and stood up. "Back here, Chels," she quietly said, motioning.

Todd looked back to see one of the prettiest strawberry blondes he'd ever seen coming toward them. With green eyes and light freckles, no less!

"Hi, everybody," she said smiling. "I hope I'm not interrupting anything."

"Your timing is perfect," Libby assured her. "We've just finished...for today anyway."

Karen, seeing the discussion wrapping up, had come over. "Are you all finished?" Nods came from all quarters. "I've been eavesdropping. You people have the coolest conversations! I catch a snippet here and there." Then she laughed. "I don't understand much of it, but it just feels good to know conversations like this go on! I'll get your checks."

Once she left, Chelsea looked over and said warmly, "Hi, Mike."

"Hey, Chelsea," Mike replied with an affectionate smile. He introduced her to Ray and Todd. Following the acknowledgments, Mike asked, "Your dad in town?"

Chelsea shook her head quietly. "But Mom's here." Then remembering, she said, "*And she's double parked!* If we're going to find any parking close to the stadium, we need to be going."

Good-byes were said, and after Eric told Libby he'd cover her breakfast once Karen brought the checks, Chelsea and Libby made their way through the crowded tables.

Todd looked back as they left and, with a bewildered smile, said, "What is it about these Christian girls? They're beautiful. They're unpretentious...and neither one has a date to the game!"

"That might be okay for Libby, if the right guy came along," Mike said with a chuckle. "But Chelsea's under house arrest and will be for some time. She can go places with her mom or someone else recognized by the court—Libby—but that's about it."

Todd's face showed surprise. Then it hit him. "*That's* the drunk?!"

Mike shook his head with quiet disapproval. "She's no drunk. In fact, she rarely drinks. But she was that night."

"Have you told him the story, Eric?" Ray asked.

"Just bits and pieces."

"Would you like to know what went down?" Mike asked Todd.

Todd nodded. "But don't you have to go?"

Mike shook his head. "I didn't have time to do justice to Ray's second question, but this won't take long. And it's important."

Chapter Four

Alone

"As a freshman," Mike began, "Chelsea joined her mother's sorority, but she told them she wasn't going to party; she was going to study, which is exactly what she did. She made the dean's list every quarter her first year—quite a feat for an incoming freshman at the University of Florida. She refused to get lost in the freshman stupidity and ended up as the designated driver for her sorority sisters most of the time. But when she got back last fall, the sorority barbeque was being held at the sorority house. She wasn't in class yet. She wasn't going out or driving anywhere, so she decided to let down a little and drink. What she didn't know was, because her sorority sisters and frat brothers had never seen her drunk, they were spiking her drinks. But again, that shouldn't have really mattered; she wasn't going out, nor would she be driving. Until her sorority big sister, Marti, came in about 9 o'clock that night and began demanding Chelsea drive her to her boyfriend's apartment; they'd had a fight."

"Why couldn't she drive herself?" Todd asked.

Mike replied, "She'd lost her own license because of a DUI.

"Anyway, Chelsea initially refused, not thinking she was in any condition to drive, but finally got bullied into doing it. Add to that, Marti got pretty animated and demanding as they began to work their way across town, telling her where to turn, which route to take and always to go *faster!* And she became increasingly louder and more excited and eventually quite caustic.

"Finally, after about ten minutes of this, Chelsea'd had enough and turned to her to tell her to shut up! And *wham!* Two people died."

Todd shook his head. "Wow. That's horrible." Then, as he collected his thoughts, he added, "So how did you get involved?"

"The lead prosecutor for the state attorney's office is on my local ministry's board," Mike said. "He has a real interest in Darwinism and what Carl and I had been doing with Eric and Libby last summer, so he knew about them both through me.

"I always told him that if he ever came across a case he felt I could help with, to let me know. He's got to be hardnosed in court—that's his job—but he does a lot behind the scenes to make sure those on trial get the support they need to learn the lessons they have to without their conviction becoming a permanent condition. He knows about programs and resources—chaplains and counselors, halfway houses, financial resources—that can get them back on track.

"In Chelsea's case, he was working closely behind the scenes with the defense team. He knew Chelsea's defense attorney personally; they're close friends. And because of what had happened, and what she was facing, she was on a suicide watch. This girl had never so much as been to the principal's office, and she was facing the probability of some significant prison time. The judge in the case had a reputation for being tough on convicted drunk drivers when a death was involved. So the prosecutor called me and asked if Libby might get involved; this girl needed a friend."

Todd nodded as he remembered a past conversation. "Eric's told me a little about this, enough to know that one of the victims was close to both Libby and him and that Libby got involved to help her—which I thought was pretty gracious. I could just never understand why."

"Well," Mike replied thoughtfully, "that's the call of the gospel, Todd, to enter in to someone else's pain, someone else's misfortune, even if that pain and misfortune have cost you. The central claim of Christianity is that God entered in to time and space, into our lives and condition, and gave himself to solve our problem— our separation from him. The term for this is incarnation; Libby decided to be incarnational, to lay aside her own interests and very painful loss, to pay the price and step into Chelsea's situation and circumstances and carry for her what she couldn't carry."

Todd shook his head quietly, a little dumbfounded. "That's like Mother Teresa."

"*Exactly.*" Mike nodded. "Just like that. I couldn't have been more proud of her. But it's who she is."

Eric then interjected, "Chelsea's talking tomorrow night at First Baptist in Alachua. One of the teachers who heard her at the

MADD[33] assembly at Santa Fe High School in Alachua set it up; the teacher goes to that church. Chelsea's not just speaking to the youth group but to the whole congregation. If you want to hear her story, we could go."

"I've got a philosophy class study group at six o'clock that goes for an hour," Todd replied.

"We could still make it," Eric responded. "We could catch the last of it, if you wanted to. I think the judge is speaking too."

Todd thought it through. "We *could* make it. Yeah, let's go."

Ray turned to Mike. "I think I'd like to hear her...and the judge too. That would be an interesting story."

"It *is* interesting to hear them together," Mike said. "The judge loves Chelsea—they've become very close—but he pulls no punches. I'll go with you, if you'd like."

Ray agreed, and they told the boys they would see them there.

By the time Todd and Eric arrived the next night, Chelsea was making her final comments. They spotted Mike and Ray closer to the front but had to slip into a pew in the back of the church.

Chelsea had shared about Libby earlier in her talk, so as she finished up she said, "Libby reminds me often of the verse in Romans, 'And we know that God causes all things to work together for good to those who love God, to those who are called according to His purpose.'[34] That's hard to see sometimes, particularly when those things are devastating losses. I knew one of the victims; Libby

---

33 Mothers Against Drunk Driving.
34 Romans 8:28.

and her family knew the other. Two people who are gone now. But, at least, one of them I know I'll see someday.

"In the meantime, what is the good he's working out? Well, for what it's worth, I was introduced to my Savior. And the person who introduced me to him has become my closest friend, my sister in Christ. My parents have come to the Lord. The judge in the case, who you will hear from next, and his wife, have both met Christ. Thousands of high school students have heard and are hearing this story—not the faith side, mind you; that's apparently against the law—but the lessons-learned side. And God is being glorified through the lives of the surviving families. Grace and forgiveness are *real* and *tangible* things to me, things I hope I can give away in the way they've been given to me.

"Thank you for the opportunity to share my story. If God can bring good out of this, then I hope you see he can bring good out of anything, and that includes anything you might be facing. Trust him to do so."

She then looked down at the front row. "Judge?"

Chelsea made her way down from the lectern and was met by a tall, older gentleman who looked as if he might be her grandfather, but everyone knew he was the judge who had sentenced her. He hugged her, and not just in passing. It was a long and affectionate hug. He then kissed her on the forehead and moved toward the podium himself.

"I love that young lady," he said tenderly. "My wife and I have no children, so we have no grandchildren. Chelsea, though, has become our unofficially adopted granddaughter. She *is* precious. But she's also a convicted felon and remains today on house arrest.

"And she *is* absolutely right: Two people are dead because of her being behind the wheel that night. And under normal circumstances—anything close to being normal—she would be in prison right now...if it hadn't been for the vigorous efforts of one of the surviving families and the believing community surrounding them.

"My standard sentence in a case involving death due to drinking is to send the person found guilty to prison. I think I owe that much to the community. But in Chelsea's case grace walked in. Grace walked in and not only saved her from prison, but also, from what the attorneys involved in the case shared with me, saved her life. The response of one of the victims' families was dumbfounding; I'd never seen anything like it. Once they got to know Chelsea and Chelsea's parents, they began to put intense pressure on me *not* to choose incarceration. They knew Chelsea was remorseful, and they knew the circumstances that put her in that car that night. They'd lost a child, but there had to be another way. In the end, no one had suffered more of a loss than they had, so I agreed. And that's why Chelsea's working with area chapters of MADD instead of being behind bars.

"But what this family did had a deep and dramatic impact on my life. Following Chelsea's sentencing hearing, once there could be no conflict of interest, I was more than a little intrigued, and I decided to go back to church, something I'd not done in years. Church had become old and formal and stilted. But when I visited the church where Chelsea was going, the church of one of the victims' families, things were anything but. And it was there I connected the dots. Not only the dots among the players—the surviving parents and the Jennings family and the attorneys, who are all evangelical Christians—but I also began to hear the story of a God who gets involved.

"Being a judge, it might be a little easier for me to relate to him in this role. I've always tried to do the honorable thing, to be the good jurist, to be evenhanded and fair, even to show mercy where mercy is due. But I've never been involved with the kind of legal case God's been handling. And what I've come to see from the gospel is something I will never see in my lifetime—perfect adjudication. Absolute justice combined with absolute love and mercy—*both* being utterly and completely satisfied.

"As I said, Chelsea is guilty. But then so am I...and so are you. In our case, the wages of what we've done is death; our 'cosmic treason,' as one theologian[35] put it, is a capital crime. But God paid the price for our sin in Christ's death on the cross—fully satisfying justice and fully allowing for mercy. I will never be on the judicial giving end as a judge of a case like that, but I am certainly on the receiving end as a defendant. I would caution all of us, though: Absolute love and mercy have been satisfied and extended to us in Christ. But there is another part to this absolute justice that is yet to be—a final, terrifying day. And I see it coming.

"Four verses after Paul's wonderful verse that Chelsea quoted—Romans 8:28—is another verse that says God 'did not spare His own Son, but delivered Him up for us all....'[36] He can give no more. He can do no more than that. So when that day comes, and all has been given that can be given, and all has been received that will be received, then there is nothing left to be dispensed but raw justice. And I will tell you, ladies and

---

35 "Cosmic treason" is a description attributed to theologian R. C. Sproul.
36 Romans 8:32.

gentlemen, when there are no extenuating circumstances, when the full guilt of the defendant is on display, then raw justice is dispensed. And it's not a pretty sight.

"The day young Chelsea Howard stood before my bench to be sentenced, she stood alone. Her sorority sister, who'd demanded to be driven across town that fateful night, wasn't there to take any of the judicial heat; she was dead. Her fraternity brothers and sorority sisters who'd spiked her drinks weren't there either. Maybe some were in the courtroom gallery, but they weren't in her shoes facing a sentence. Neither was her mother nor her dad, nor Libby Jennings, nor the victim's family, who'd worked so hard on her behalf. Only Chelsea stood there. Only Chelsea sat in the driver's seat that night and put on her seatbelt and started the car. Only the one responsible for doing that is ultimately responsible for the results and is the court responsible for adjudicating. She stood alone before the bench, as we all will.

"One day I will stand alone before the Judge in my case. I'm thankful I've been told of and received his free gift of pardon and eternal life, extended to me by the death and resurrection of his Son. I cannot imagine standing before him otherwise, having dismissed his gift—alone with nowhere to turn and no one to turn to.

"Tonight put your life in the hands of the One who has spared no expense to save you. Don't face that day on your own without Christ. He did it so you wouldn't have to. He gave his life to purchase our pardon. If you refuse his gift, if you ignore his grace, then all that is left is raw justice. I'm convinced this is what the author of the book of Hebrews was alluding to when he said, 'It is a terrifying thing to fall into the hands of the living God.'[37]

"Trust him. He is a Judge like no other.

"Thank you for allowing us to tell you our story."

---

37   Hebrews 10:31.

Chapter Five

The Professor's Questions

Ray and Mike were the first to the Skillet the following week and were sipping their coffees when the now four students arrived.

"Chelsea was hoping she could be a fly-on-the-wall," Libby said. "These two are okay with it," she added, nodding in the direction of Eric and Todd. "You don't mind, do you?"

Mike and Ray looked at each other and expressed their agreement. Mike added, "Sure. But you have to understand, Chelsea, this is a theoretical conversation, and in it Christianity is fair game. We're wrestling with a philosophical subject, so some observations about our faith might be a bit blunt."

She nodded. "I'm just here to listen in."

Ray then said to Chelsea, "That was one heck of a story you shared last Sunday. Very powerful. And the judge is quite a preacher. If I hadn't had my wits about me, I might've gotten born again."

"I don't think it was your wits that got in the way," Chelsea replied softly. "Let's just hope that whatever it was, you find a way around it. We all need saving."

Ray smiled and looked at Mike, who knew exactly what he was thinking: pretty, unpretentious *and frank*. Today could be interesting.

The conversations then began among everyone, and the interesting points of the week were shared, including the University of Florida's victory the week before. They also gave Karen their orders for breakfast.

Ray then mentioned how much he had enjoyed the discussion the previous week—that he felt the issue they'd discussed had been dealt with thoroughly and intelligently—no sidestepping or shell games. But he also said that because of his daughter's ongoing condition, and the academic work he was having to do for an advanced degree, this morning would probably be his last chance to get together on the topic of evil.

Todd chuckled and said he might have a couple of questions that would probably torpedo the whole discussion. "I had a chance to talk to my philosophy professor this past week. I told him I'd been meeting with some true believers—three 'born again' Christians and a Jewish person—to discuss if morality and moral values were objective or not. He said he thought that sounded a bit like 'the fox guarding the henhouse' and that the last people I needed to be talking to about morality, if I wanted to keep my brain cells from being toasted, were born-again Christians."

Ray's expression turned sour. "I don't consider myself a true believer, as you put it, but I can certainly respect people of faith. And I also know plenty of free thinkers, but I steer clear of the cocky ones. It sounds like your prof is plenty full of himself."

"He is," Todd agreed. "He's a good teacher, though—he certainly keeps us entertained—but I don't go along with his attitude. For one thing, I know Eric and Libby…and I don't know anyone like Eric and Libby. I might see the world through the professor's lenses, but I'm not at all sure I'd want one populated by people like him. I think I'd rather it be made up of folks like these two," as he nodded in the direction of the Jennings siblings. "What they did last year involving Chelsea…this world needs people like that."

"That it does," Chelsea agreed.

Todd smiled at Chelsea's agreement and then continued, "Anyway…he *did* have a couple of questions for you, and I think they're good ones. Can we take a look at them?" Mike nodded quietly, not quite sure where this would take them, as Todd pulled a paper out of his pocket. "He said to ask this one first, and if you could get past it, to ask the second. Ready?"

Mike smiled at the challenge. So Todd read from his note, "Is what is moral loved by God because it's moral, or is it moral because it's loved by God?"

Ray turned to Mike with a knowing smile. "That's a cleverly articulated problem. I guess that's supposed to create some sort of issue for you. We know the philosophy professor would like it to."

Mike nodded. "It was a question originally asked by Socrates— different time, different circumstances. Its current rendering is designed to impale the theist on the horns of a dilemma. If we answer yes to the first half of the question—is what is moral loved by God because it's moral—then we admit that moral values and duties have their own intrinsic value, and we don't need God to tell us what that is. And God is out of a job; he would be irrelevant when it comes to morality. This was Socrates' position, by the way, and is the position of the secular culture now and, I'd imagine, Todd's professor.

"On the other hand, if we say yes to the second half of the question, then the charge is that moral values and obligations are essentially based on God's personal whims—His capriciousness. And arbitrary whims should never be considered a valid basis for sound moral valuation. Either way the theist's or believer's position is deemed disposed of."

Ray nodded his understanding. Seeing how familiar Mike was with the problem, and knowing he had probably given this a good deal of thought, he relaxed and watched, confident his Christian friend was up to the challenge.

"So," Mike said to Todd, "do you know under what circumstances this question originated—why it was asked?"

"I've never heard it before," Todd admitted.

"You'll need to know that," Mike responded, "if you're going to fully understand the problem. If we don't know why it was first stated, we won't see why it might or might not apply to our current discussions.

"The question Socrates posed is found in Plato's *dialogues*. It's part of a conversation Socrates had with an Athenian of some reputation as Socrates prepared for his own trial. He was charged with leading the youth of Athens into 'impiety.'"

"And that was a serious charge?" Ray asked.

Mike nodded assuredly. "Socrates was training a student body to think critically. As part of that training, the students were taught to question anything and everything including the stories about the Greek gods. To Socrates, the stories were suspicious and inconsistent; he found them hard to swallow. This apparently didn't sit well with the Athenians who felt that if Socrates ticked the gods off, all would not go well for Athens. Bringing him to trial was somewhat like bringing a Jew to trial for blasphemy; it was a capital offense."

"Just for doubting," Todd said dismissively. "How stupid!"

"You mean like expressing doubts about Darwin in front of someone like Richard Dawkins?" Mike quipped.

Todd looked at Mike a bit surprised as he recognized how universal the experience is of crossing someone else's belief system and the ire that can create. He hadn't realized this before.

"Anyway," Mike continued, "to construct a defense, Socrates had to first determine what the courts meant by impiety. And no one seemed to know. This resulted in his conversation with Euthyphro, a citizen known for his expertise in religious and ethical matters. Euthyphro happened to be in the court environs bringing his father up on charges of manslaughter because he had failed to give proper care to a slave in his charge who subsequently died. Socrates was very impressed with Euthyphro—seeing that the man was so consistent in his handling of ethical matters that he'd charge his own father in a case like this—and felt sure he'd be able to give him a clear definition of what was pious or impious and therefore a basis to construct his own defense. But it didn't work out that way.

"Every time Euthyphro attempted to define what was or wasn't pious, Socrates showed it to be an incomplete or inconsistent or self-contradictory answer. Socrates finally asked this question: 'Is what is pious loved by the gods because it's pious, or is it pious because it's loved by the gods?' What the professor has asked is simply a restatement of this problem. It's known as the Euthyphro dilemma."

"So how do you answer it?" Eric asked.

"There are a couple of ways," Mike replied. "The first is to do a thought experiment. Let's say God loves what is good or moral because it's just that—good or moral. This means we don't need God to give us its value; we don't need God period. So God is of no moral consequence. We have no transcendent Lawgiver to whom we can appeal *or to whom we are accountable*.

"By the way, those two go hand-in-hand. If we're going to have Someone to whom we can appeal as an arbiter in such matters, that same Someone must be able to enforce those standards and to hold us accountable if we fail to do so. Otherwise, having objective moral duties is simply academic.

"What we're finding in the professor's world today—our secular culture at large—is just that; having dispensed with God we've dispensed with any consequences; there is no *fear of God* left. We have people out there who are messed in the head and think: 'I'm getting tired of my life—it's going nowhere—so maybe I should exit now. And, gee, wouldn't it be exciting to create my own send-off? Like the grand finale at the Fourth of July fireworks display where they all go off at once? Since there is no God who's going to judge me, all I really need to worry about are the cops. And if I just save the last bullet for me, I can turn my world into a video game and use real ammo. I can take out probably twenty-five or thirty people before turning the gun around. Whoopee!" Mike shook his head at the disturbing thought. "The killers at Columbine, the shooter in the Golden, Colorado movie theatre and the killer in Newtown would all fit this mold. Just one consequence of an 'enlightened,' *secular* culture."

Then he continued, "The rational problem is this: unless there is a Higher Authority to whom we can appeal and to whom we are accountable—the transcendent Moral Lawgiver—and things are seen as having their own intrinsic value, who's to say *whose recognition or valuation* of those intrinsic moral values is the correct one? On what is this valuation based? How is mine better than yours? How would Mother Teresa's valuation be better than, say, Saddam Hussein's? Or Joseph Stalin's? Or Mao Tse Tung's? And so we find these objective moral values and obligations are now based upon *our* whims and capriciousness instead of God's. And this means they are no longer objective; they are subjective. And a world of these kinds of moral frameworks can be a dangerous place. It's fine so long as you're on the right side of everyone else's moral values, but if you are seen as an unvalued member—an unborn child or maybe an invalid or someone who is old, feeble and sickly…or, as we saw in Nazi Germany, being Jewish—things might get a bit dicey for you.

"The second is this: The issue for Socrates *was* an either/or problem, and that made his question valid when he asked it. Why? Because the gods of the ancient Greeks *were* petty and capricious, arbitrary and whimsical. They were the anthropomorphic projections of the Greeks; they were imaginary! But can the same be said for the *uncreated* God of Judaism and Christianity? I don't think so, and I have sound reasons for this, but that's a different discussion.

"God is assumed, in the modern restatement of this problem, to be petty, arbitrary and capricious, and so His valuations of what are good or moral are seen as suspect. But why is this so? How is it that our secularist is willing to allow that some*thing* can be good or moral in and of itself, as in the first argument, but not Some*one*? And what if this Some*one* was truly all-loving, all-powerful, all-knowing and morally perfect? Wouldn't that make Him the foundation—the measure—of all that is good and moral?"

Mike looked at Eric's roommate. "Todd…?"

Todd just smiled a surrender; he had no response.

"Christian philosophers have seen the issues raised by Euthyphro for a long time but have recognized the rational problem when applying the argument to the God of the Bible. Their position is simply that objective moral values and duties are an extension—an expression or a reflection—of God's good and holy *nature* for the reasons we discussed last week. Without his moral nature—the straightedge—neither the good and the holy nor the possibility of the evil or profane exist. He is truly the *measure* of all things good—and by consequence, bad—and by which all of those things are *defined*."

Things got quiet. This was a lot to take in.

Ray nodded that Mike's answer seemed sufficient for him. Eric, Libby and Chelsea looked at each other with quiet smiles; Mike had handled things well enough. At this point, Karen delivered the breakfast orders. Once they all made it to the proper patron, Ray looked at Todd. "But you had a second question, didn't you?"

"Oh, yeah." Todd smiled. "Mike's swinging for the fences, so let's see what he can do with this one."

"The Bible says Adam and Eve were created good. So how does something created good choose something evil?"

"What's so hard about that?" Libby asked. Eric was quiet; it was the same question he'd asked Todd earlier when Todd had shared the two challenges with him.

Mike said, "It's more difficult than it might seem. That's a question honest scholars have wrestled with, some with more success than others."

Todd smiled. "Yeah, he said so. He said he reads born-again Christian scholars like some people read Calvin and Hobbes. He used to be a Lutheran or something, but he got tired of being associated with anything Christian. He still likes to read stuff from what he calls the dark side, though. He says it's fodder for his philosophy class."

"Sounds like your professor really has it in for anyone who's a believer in anything," Ray observed.

"He can include himself in that group," Mike replied. "The professor believes plenty."

Todd shook his head. "He's an atheist."

"We'll come back to what atheists believe," Mike assured him. "But right now we need to address his second challenge. As we did last week, and then again just now addressing Euthyphro, we need to remember that a central component in the whole idea of objective moral obligations is that it's 'the mere existence of the standard or value that automatically and inescapably creates the potential for its own violation.' So if we're dealing with real moral values, we're dealing with a universe whose basis is God. And if we're dealing with God, we're going to have to engage Genesis as somehow historical— that it can give us some *true* insights into the original problem. It's the only theistic story we in the West have. To his credit, the professor seems to see this—he used the term 'created'—and has opened things up. So let's have at it.

"The question the philosophy professor is raising is problematic because, theoretically, the idea is that our original fall should have been impossible. It's assumed by some scholars that Adam and Eve were initially *morally good* moral agents. We know that because of the juxtaposition of good with evil in the question itself. But is it true they were? If so, then here is where the conundrum presents itself. How does something created morally good choose something evil? If the professor's really read these Christian scholars, he understands that a driving premise behind the question is that we only do what we are *inclined* to do.[38] So a morally good moral agent would only be inclined to choose the good. If the assumption about Adam and Eve being created this way is correct, then the question is, in reality, unanswerable, which is why he's asked it."

"So what *is* the answer?" Ray asked, confident by now that his friend had probably studied this and wasn't stumped.

Mike replied, "It has to do with unpacking the underlying assumptions. There are two issues here: one is what kind of good are we talking about when referring to Adam and Eve—was this good a moral good? And the other has to do with the choosing of something evil, so the answer to this is twofold."

Everyone nodded that they were clear on the starting assumptions. Mike then said, "First, I'd suggest they weren't created *morally* good. Their initial condition was innocent; they had no inclination to choose good or evil. Scholars I've read seem to think the choice in the garden was limited to a moral one, but is that so? Like you said last week, Ray, you can choose breakfast here or go to the grocery store and make any number of choices that have no moral implications whatsoever. And, initially, that was their situation; they had no moral choices to make."

---

38   R. C. Sproul, *Reason to Believe: A Response to Common Objections to Christianity*,
      Zondervan Publishing House, 1982, pp. 124-125.

"No moral choices to make?" Libby asked.

"Remember," Mike replied, "originally, there were no prohibitions in the garden; there was no way to fail. In the first chapter of Genesis, God told them he'd given them '*every* plant yielding seed....'[39] The tree of the knowledge of good and evil wasn't yet on the radar. With that being the case, morality was a moot issue; initially no prohibitions. . .so no wrong choices and no way to mess up in any moral sense."

"But it did become an issue, Mike," Libby said. "And what about the fact that God created them 'very good'?[40] I mean, we're made in God's image,[41] and God is certainly moral if he's anything."

"Yeah," Eric said. "Doesn't Paul say in Romans...?" He looked for the passage on his smartphone.

> For when the Gentiles who do not have the Law do *instinctively* the things of the Law, these, not having the Law are a law to themselves in that they show the work of the Law *written in their hearts*, their conscience bearing witness, and their thoughts alternately accusing or else defending them.[42]

Mike grew thoughtful. "I think we can all agree that the Bible says we were made in God's image, but just what that entails is open to massive debate. God is omnipotent, omniscient, omnipresent and timeless, and we are none of those things; being made in his image didn't extend to those characteristics. So our having an

---

39   Genesis 1:29 (emphasis mine).
40   Genesis 1:31.
41   Genesis 1:26.
42   Romans 2:14-15 (emphasis mine).

intrinsic moral nature from the get-go can be no more than an assumption. One of the problems with that idea is answering what role the tree of the knowledge of good and evil played in our lives. Something dramatic happened when we ate from the tree. We immediately saw things differently. And we need to ask why that was and what it tells us."

Eric and Libby were stopped by Mike's observation.

"On the other hand, if Adam and Eve made the choice *before* they received that intrinsic moral nature—if this inward inscription of God's Law on their hearts was done *after* the choice, by the tree itself—the playing field is very different, and good takes on a different meaning."

"How so?" Todd asked.

"Well…a Hellfire or Maverick guided missile is considered a good weapon because it can destroy an enemy target with remarkable precision, but it's not good in any moral sense. Heroin or cocaine that's ninety-nine percent pure is as good as it gets without being in a sterile environment; yet being moral has nothing to do with this description either. These are examples of things that are good in the substantial or essential sense that there is little or nothing compromising *what* they are.

"Let's look at that first chapter in Genesis." Mike pulled up the chapter in the Bible app on his tablet. "In the first chapter of Genesis, 'good' is used in verses 4, 10, 12, 18, 21 and 25, but at no time is it used as a moral description. Light, dry land, vegetation, the sun and moon, aquatic and avian life forms, and all other animal species are all described as good; yet none can be understood as having any moral capacity or responsibility whatsoever. Even when 'very good' is used in verse 31, it is as a summary description including mankind along with everything else. Good, again, is being used in the ontological as opposed to moral sense. With this in mind, let's revisit the question.

"Some believe Adam and Eve first became moral by eating from the tree of the knowledge of good and evil. The problem with this assumption is that it seems they could not be held morally accountable for choices *before* eating from the tree, and this would include their choice to eat from the tree itself. Yet for what were they judged? Their crime was, in fact, the *act* of eating from the tree, not for what the tree imparted, so their moral accountability had to precede their encounter with the tree. Others believe mankind, again, being made in God's image, was created as a good moral agent with an intrinsic moral nature from the very first moment. This would answer the issue of moral accountability, but then the scholars' question seems unsolvable. Indeed, how could they fall? In the words of your professor, Todd, how could something created good choose something evil? Both have what appear to be insurmountable problems."

"So there has to be a third option," Ray surmised.

Mike nodded. "If the problem is to be answered, there must be.

"The case can be made that mankind went through a three-fold progression. We were created good, but this was only an ontological good; there was nothing to compromise what we were—rational and free. We became morally *accountable* the moment the tree was identified and the prohibition was given. Once that took place, a standard was erected or identified that could either be embraced or violated by a rational, free creature, and the moral dimension was added to a universe that previously had no possibility for either success or failure, good or evil. Adam and Eve knew that eating from the tree was wrong—the prohibition said so—and it is on this basis they were judged. Finally, we received our intrinsic moral nature—our innate conscience—by eating from the tree of the knowledge of good and evil itself. It was in eating from the tree that we saw what nakedness was. It was only by the tree that God's Law was written *on our hearts*, that our moral accountability progressed from an external command to a natural[43] intuition—what you just shared, Eric, from Romans. So one answer to the question of how a good creature could make the choice it did depends on *which* good we were *when* the choice was made. This, of course, brings us back to what we were talking about last week: what God can and can't do."

Todd chuckled. "My favorite subject…"

"Knowledge and nature are not the same things," Mike said, smiling in response. "Being free and knowing the good is not the same as being free and always choosing the good. Creating a rational agent with moral capacity is not the same as creating a *morally good* moral agent. Is the creation of the latter even possible—a being that is not only rational and free but, at the same time, one that would always choose the good and never the alternative? We know of only one Being who is fundamentally good in this sense—both free and who forever chooses the good. That kind of inherent quality might be an attribute that is unique to God alone. If this is the case, it would mean that *creating* an innately good moral agent out of whole cloth is as impossible as creating an infinite creature, or any number of other absurdities—smelling the color nine, as one songwriter[44] put it. Of course, creating is not God's only option. There are other

---

43   Knowing good and evil became ours by nature, an integral part of the human psyche.

44   Chris Rice, *Short Term Memories* album.

means to this end, which actually we'll deal with when we get to Ray's second question.

"By the way, Todd," Mike added, "the other half of your professor's question has an answer, too. Eve didn't choose anything evil. The tree of the knowledge of good and evil wasn't evil. God doesn't make evil things; He makes things that can be misused and can therefore end up corrupted. In fact, the reason Eve chose the fruit was because she saw its *good* benefits. If you read the passage in Genesis,[45] she runs through the list; she was *thinking* this through—pleasing to the eye...good for food... would make you wise.... This wasn't a choice between good or evil—a moral choice. This was a rational decision. Where it went awry was that when she chose *for* something—the fruit— she chose *against* another—obeying God's command. In other words, she didn't choose anything evil; she made an evil choice. There's a difference. Part of the problem is in the framing of the question itself."

All saw Mike's point and nodded in agreement. But then a curious expression appeared on Todd's face. "So if the tree was all that good, why the prohibition? Why would God want to keep it from us...or us from it?"

Mike grew thoughtful. "Any answer is just speculation, but one thought is that the tree would somehow give us the knowledge without the attending ability—too much sail, too shallow a keel; too big a gun for the beam."

"Come again?" Chelsea asked.

Mike smiled to himself; he'd just used a 'guy' analogy. "Back when our biggest weapons were guns and cannons—sixteen-inch

45   Genesis 3:6.

diameter shells with a range of more than twenty miles—they mounted them on battleships. And for them to work they gave the ship a very wide beam. Otherwise, the first time they'd fired a broadside, they'd have capsized." While saying this, he made a quick circling motion with his finger showing the ship rolling over.

"You have to admit, a great human frustration is our recognition of and desire to do good—the right thing—but we find ourselves invariably choosing otherwise. Humanists therefore appeal to the innate goodness of man because of what we *want* to do, but theologians see things differently. They believe mankind is fundamentally flawed because of where we actually go, what we actually end up doing—our incessant inability to put into practice what we know we should do. Paul talked about this very clearly in the seventh chapter of his epistle to the Romans."

Ray then said to Todd, "I don't suppose your professor would have thought his challenges could have been deconstructed like this."

"Nor did I," Todd admitted.

Ray turned to Mike. "Do you often come across people as dismissive as the professor?"

"A lot, really," Mike said. "To people like that, religious belief is synonymous with irrationality. To them, it's quite impossible for a believer in God to be scientific or logical or anything close. They're quite naïve. And I find that people like that are usually oblivious to their own *massive*, faith commitments."

Todd interjected, "Like I said before, he has *no* faith commitments. He's an atheist."

"That's what I mean, Todd," Mike responded. "Your professor thinks faith only comes into play in a religious context when dealing with belief in some kind of deity, but that's not the case. It's the assumptions he uses to put together his picture of the world. And anything not *absolutely* known is believed."

"Come again?"

"Unless we're dealing with a rigorous proof in mathematics, or something self-evident or true by definition—triangles have three sides, bachelors are not married—or a perfect induction where all elements in question can be known"—Mike picked up the plastic stand-up menu in the middle of the table to clarify—"all the ink used on this Specials of the Day menu is black—we're dealing with unknowns. And it's those unknowns that require faith in some way."

"I'm still not following you," Todd said.

Mike tried again. "Let's say you're called to jury duty, and both sides present their case, but the prosecution's case is much stronger. You weren't an eyewitness to the crime, but he builds such a compelling case for the defendant's guilt that, once sequestered, everyone on the jury agrees the accused is guilty beyond a reasonable doubt. Well, what does that mean?"

"You're far more confident he's guilty than he's innocent."

"Exactly," Mike answered. "You've seen how the different lines of evidence fit together and they all converge; they all point in one direction. But you don't *know;* you weren't there. Again you weren't an eyewitness. So the accused's guilt is not based on absolute proof. It's based on converging lines of evidence that can only take you back so far, can only get you so close to the crime being committed, can only get you so close to absolute proof, but not fully. You must then make an informed decision now to fill in the final steps based on the convergence of that evidence. And *informed decisions based on converging lines of evidence are what evangelical Christians mean by faith.* There is nothing that shows more ignorance on the part of the atheist for their counterparts than to think that faith is something you have when you have no evidence. It's anything but.

"Your philosophy professor wasn't there when the universe began or when the earth was formed, didn't see how the first life came to be, nor has he seen how life has developed since then. He has lines of evidence he *interprets* to come up with a picture he *believes* to be true. He has certain assumptions that contribute to the assembling of this evidence—that life is basically a material phenomenon and that God or a god wasn't involved. But he doesn't *know* that in any absolute sense; he can only believe. And if he's honest he'll admit that, whatever his evidence might be, he's having to fill in an awful lot. And it's those fill-in-the-blanks that are his faith commitments.

"It isn't whether or not he believes in God but that he *believes* anything at all. And he has to if he's going to operate in the real world and not spend his life in a rubber room."

Todd nodded. "I see your point."

Mike then took a moment to make it more personal. "There's one other thing to keep in mind here, Todd, and it has to do with the attitude of the heart. Like I mentioned to you the first time we talked, any great idea making great claims or that carries great consequences should be thoroughly cross-examined. And this requires a certain level of skepticism. A *healthy* skepticism allows you to investigate something soberly and intelligently but also allows for you to change your position if a level of evidence arises that compels you to do so. There's nothing wrong with that. But there's another level of skepticism that's counterproductive—a *hardened* skepticism, an attitude that won't allow for a change of mind no matter what level of evidence presents itself. A hardened skepticism cares only for its own position; the truth is irrelevant. It's the mindset of the fundamentalist whether they be backwoods Bible-thumpers or Harvard biologists.[46] I'm afraid this is the camp your philosophy professor might be in. I hope it's not the case with you."

"Amen to that," Ray agreed.

Eric, Libby and Chelsea looked at Ray with surprise and laughed. Ray shrugged a smile and said, "What…? Jewish agnostics can say amen when they agree with something." Mike and Todd joined in the fun too, recognizing why the three had reacted that way.

Ray then asked, "So, with all that being said, can we address the second question? I'm not going to be able to come back, and I'd like to see where we go with it."

"That's right where we're going," Mike answered.

"Can we restate the question?" Libby asked.

Mike looked at Ray encouragingly, so Ray read….

---

46 An example of hardened skepticism would be that shown by Harvard Professor Richard Lewontin in his review of Carl Sagan's *The Demon-Haunted World: Science as a Candle in the Dark*, New York Review of Books, January 9, 1997: "We take the side of science in spite of the patent absurdity of some of its constructs, in spite of its failure to fulfill many of its extravagant promises of health and life, in spite of the tolerance of the scientific community for unsubstantiated just-so stories, because we have a prior commitment, a commitment to materialism. It is not that the methods and institutions of science somehow compel us to accept a material explanation of the phenomenal world, but on the contrary, that we are forced by our *a priori* adherence to material causes to create an apparatus of investigation and a set of concepts that produce material explanations, no matter how counter-intuitive, no matter how mystifying to the uninitiated. Moreover, that materialism is absolute, for we cannot allow a Divine Foot in the door."

Chapter Six

The Tale of Two Timeframes

"How is it that God seemingly sits so idly by as evil and suffering ravage what he's made?"

Mike stayed quiet for a moment to allow the question to sink in. Then he offered, "Let's make some assumptions. The most important is that the God we are dealing with is, as was just stated, all-knowing, all-powerful, all-loving and perfectly moral. The answer will be found without compromising any of these attributes.

"And if I can, let me offer a couple of approaches scholars have taken before in answering this question," he continued. "One is called the soul-building theodicy.[47] This explanation simply

---

[47] This theodicy is attributed to Iranaeus (130-202), Bishop of Lugdunum in Gaul (now Lyons, France).

claims certain attributes and character traits cannot be brought about in us by anything other than adverse circumstances. As the saying goes, a diamond is simply a piece of coal that stuck to the job. Without the pressure it would never become hard or beautiful or valuable."

"So now you're saying evil is necessary?" Todd asked.

Mike grew thoughtful. "More that its inevitability has positive applications. Chelsea knows love, grace and forgiveness at a level few of us ever will; they are tangible realities to her. And her ability to give back now, particularly to people carrying a lot of guilt or dealing with regret, far exceeds anything she could have developed on her own. Libby knows now that when the hard chips fall she can step it up and do just about anything God asks of her. And Eric knows he can emotionally handle pretty much any inexplicable circumstance, no matter how hard the loss, and still stay the course. I know the same thing having experienced the loss of my own mother to cancer. These are lessons learned in the crucible. So for God to make human beings of value, and that means human beings of character, they must be tested."

"So you're saying evil *has to* exist in some way for this soul-building to take place?" Todd restated his comment. He wanted to make sure he was hearing Mike correctly.

"It's hard to say yes to that," Mike replied. "Does God utilize it to accomplish things not possible otherwise? It appears so. There is simply no other way for this kind of character building to take place. C. S. Lewis spoke to this, after going through the loss of his own wife to cancer, how God uses adversity to work things deep into us." Finding the quote on his tablet, he read:

The terrible thing is that a perfectly good God is…hardly less formidable than a Cosmic Sadist. The more we believe that God hurts only to heal, the less we can believe that there is any use in begging for tenderness. A cruel man might be bribed—might grow tired of his vile sport—might have a temporary fit of mercy, as alcoholics have fits of sobriety. But suppose that what you are up against is a surgeon whose intentions are wholly good. The kinder and more conscientious he is, the more inexorably he will go on cutting. If he yielded to your entreaties, if he stopped before the operation was complete, all the pain up to that point would have been useless.[48]

"But you see the problem with this explanation, Mike," Ray said. "I would agree that character development needs opposite pressure to develop just like strength training requires resistance to build muscle, but there's lots of evil out there that never results in this kind of character building or anything close to it. It's the evil and devastation that can't be calculated. And it happens to non-rational creatures that would never benefit from any kind of moral or character enhancement. They die in droughts; they die of starvation; they die while being eaten alive by something one or two steps up the food chain. Is God allowing all of this horrible devastation to the vast biosphere just so he can teach you and me life lessons? Come on…!"

Mike nodded in honest agreement. "The soul-building theodicy is one of two explanations, and it's been recognized as insufficient

---

48 A GRIEF OBSERVED by C.S. Lewis copyright © Pte. Ltd. 1961
    C.S. Lewis, *A Grief Observed*, London, Faber and Faber LTD, 1961, pp. 55-56

to account for the big picture for the very reason you've mentioned. Insufficient as it may be in that role, we needed to explore it and to agree there are certain things—invaluable things—that simply cannot be brought about without trial. Evil doesn't exist in heaven, so if God is going to work something deep into our character, which is what soul-building means, now would be the time and place. In fact, the author of the Epistle to the Hebrews tells us that something profound was given to Christ through his mortal experience,[49] So this theodicy is not without merit; it's a legitimate explanation. It just lacks explanatory scope. We need something more to address the big picture."

Then Mike continued. "The second is known as the free-will theodicy. This is a more complete explanation; at least it has been accepted as such since Augustine. It's fallen out of favor in the past two hundred years though and needs us to do some groundwork.

"You see, again, we find ourselves on the threshold of a conundrum. Either we live in a moral universe with truly objective moral values and obligations given by a moral Lawgiver to whom we can appeal and to whom we are accountable, or we don't. If it's the latter, then this whole conversation is, again, just academic. But that's not the tack we've been taking. We're involved in this conversation, I think, because we are all convinced that we indeed live in a moral universe. So I have a question for you, Ray."

---

49   Hebrews 4:15-16, 5:8-9, 7:26 and 12:2. Yet Hebrews 13:8 tells us that "Jesus Christ *is* the same yesterday and today, *yes* and forever." As the divine second person of the triune God, he is immutable (unchangeable). How can Someone who is perfect be made more perfect? One way to understand this might be to see it like the time-lapse photography on a rosebud opening in the sunlight. The incarnation, Christ's mortal experience becoming the God/man, and his trials, temptations and suffering, appeared to allow for a fuller blooming, causing him to identify with us and our limitations more profoundly.

Ray looked at Mike a bit surprised that he should become the focus.

"Did Eric's cross-examination of Darwinism in your classroom last year erode your confidence in the theory?"

Ray grew thoughtful as he allowed the question to sink in. The three students, who knew the history involved in the question, sat rock-still waiting to see where this would go. Not knowing anything about it, Chelsea just watched. Finally Ray looked at Mike as if realizing something for the first time and began to nod quietly.

"You're not serious," Todd said. He was concerned that the one ally he had was losing his grip on reason.

"I think I'm still a Darwinist," Ray finally said. "To be anything—a design theorist or a creationist or a Darwinist—I believe you have to be able to make a positive case for your position. I guess I've viewed Darwinism and science as synonymous for so long, it's hard for me to see myself as anything but. And of those three I still believe a case can be better made for Darwin, but it's a bit more limited than it used to be."

"You're giving up on science, man…!" Todd was not going quietly.

Ray smiled. That was what he used to tell his students about Intelligent Design. Then he looked at the young ballplayer. "Am I? Do you know how the gene expression system works, Todd?"

Todd nodded tentatively.

"The reader—the RNA polymerase," Ray continued, "is directed to the initiation site of the gene, reads it, copies it and sends the transcript off to the ribosome to be translated and manufactured into a protein. So here's the question: The ribosome is itself made up of a number of proteins. Where did *those* proteins come from? We need a ribosome to make the proteins in the first place—to translate the mRNA transcript into the sequence of amino acids that the protein is built of. So what came first, the protein-building machine made of proteins or the proteins the protein-building machine is made of?"

Todd had no answer.

Ray was quiet for a moment—he didn't want to look like he was beating up on Todd—but then he continued. "Did you and Eric talk about his view on whale evolution this past week?"

Todd nodded. "And Libby."

"And what did you think?" Ray asked.

Todd shrugged. "I'm no expert on whale evolution, so I really couldn't say, but it sounded like a good argument against it."

"It's an excellent argument against it," Ray answered. "And I don't know if there is an answer out there to debunk Behe's irreducible complexity, but Kenneth Miller doesn't have it. Not for me, anyway—not anymore. And with the recent mapping of the chimpanzee Y-chromosome, human-chimpanzee common descent is no longer a slam-dunk.[50]

"Morphological similarities show a remarkable interrelatedness for nature, even hierarchies, but Linnaeus recognized that long before Darwin. And those hierarchies line up very well with the molecular and genetic evidence, so that's a plus for Darwinism. I think the fossil record also makes a strong case for evolution of some kind—it shows a progression from the simpler to the more complex, the primitive to the more modern. But then we have

---

50 For comprehensive treatments of this subject, see Jonathan Wells, *The Myth of Junk DNA*, Appendix: The Vitamin C Pseudogene, Seattle, Discovery Institute Press, 2011, and Ann Gauger, Douglas Axe and Casey Luskin, *Science and Human Origins*, Seattle, Discovery Institute Press, 2012.

virtually *nothing* prior to the Cambrian boundary. Why is that? It's a question I've skated over for years, but I can't anymore. And then Stephen Meyer points out that in *every* circumstance where we come across meaningful information—information used to communicate—we always and forever accept it to be a product of reason. Except when we find it in biology—in living systems. Why so? It's another question I've glossed over, but now I find it's front and center.

"So, yeah, Todd," Ray admitted, "maybe I am being unscientific...by somebody's definition somewhere. But, perhaps for the first time, I'm being honest with myself."

Libby and Eric could hardly believe their ears. This was something they'd been praying for. Mike was trying to be really nonchalant about things, too, but he'd been covering this ground with Ray for years. To hear Ray say he was now open to considering another story was huge.

So Mike asked his friend, "You've read the materials I've sent you on the historical case for Christ's resurrection, right?" Ray nodded. "Do you see them as at all compelling?"

"Yeah," Ray smiled to himself. "I was blown away. I had no idea a miracle could be so well substantiated from an historic or rational standpoint."

"So would you see the resurrection more as plausible, possible or probable?"

Ray grew thoughtful for a moment, smiling to himself. "That lawyer buddy of mine—the one I told you had investigated Jesus' trial?—he's quite serious about his Jewish heritage, but he's also a very honest thinker. He doesn't shy away from things. So I gave him the stuff from both organizations—*Jews for Jesus* and

Jews for Judaism—and I also gave him your information on the resurrection. He got back to me after going through it, and his response was surprising."

"Tell me…."

Ray nodded. "He said he found the Christian case for Jesus being the Messiah compelling." He smiled and shook his head recalling the conversation. Apparently it was something he wanted to remember. "He went on to say, 'We Jews have a propensity for oops-ing.'"

"Oops-ing?" the two girls giggled.

Ray nodded. "Yeah. The entire Old Testament is the story of Jewish oops-ing. Our getting sideways with God seemed to be the rule instead of the exception. Moses spends too much time on the mountain, so we make a golden calf. *Oops.* We get to the threshold of the Promised Land and send the spies in. Two come back with a good report, but ten disagree, and we choose to follow the ten. *Oops.* So we spend forty years in the desert working that one off. We take the land, but then we keep forgetting our side of the bargain. So the judges have to be sent every generation or so to keep us on track. *Oops, oops and oops.* Then we get tired of the judges and ask for a king. Not a choice God was particularly happy about. *Oops again.* The Old Testament is replete with our oops-ing; the prophets are a constant reminder of that.

"He said he doesn't think it's a genetic thing with the Jews. If the French or the Libyans or the Chinese had been chosen, they'd have acted just as stupidly. It's more of a human thing. But the Jews were chosen, so our story is the one on display. And then he wondered out loud if we hadn't oops-ed with Jesus. Had we missed it with him? He's still studying it."

"And you…?" Mike asked.

Ray shrugged. "I don't know…. Is the 'anointed one' in Daniel[51] who was 'cut off' the same as the Son of Man two chapters earlier?[52] And is this Jesus? Are the pierced hands and feet the psalmist talked about [53] a picture of him crucified? Is Isaiah's suffering servant[54] or the pierced victim in Zechariah, Christ?"[55]

Everyone was quiet; they saw how much Ray was working through. Then Mike quietly asked again, "And the resurrection, Ray? Plausible…probable…?"

Ray grew even more thoughtful. Then, looking at Mike as if he'd again allowed himself for the first time to accept the true import of what he'd been studying, he said, "I'd have to say it was a probable. There's no other way I can look at the argument or the data as we know it and come away with any other position—not rationally anyway. No other explanation addresses the breadth of the problem as well. They all fall short."

Mike took a breath before continuing. "Do you see what's going on here, Ray? If there are solid reasons to question Darwinism, and equally or even more compelling reasons to believe in Christ's bodily resurrection, then we are moving from a materialistic, purposeless, non-moral universe to a supernatural, purposeful, moral one. It's a night and day change; the differences couldn't be more profound."

Ray quietly nodded that he was on board, but Todd shook his head slowly, not believing the turn in the direction of their conversation or the loss of his ally.

---

51   Daniel 9:26.
52   Daniel 7:13-14.
53   Psalm 22:16.
54   Isaiah 53: 3-12.
55   Zechariah 12:10.

"If the resurrection is true," Mike added, "then we can know there is a God. We can know what he is like and how we can relate to him. We also have a solid substantiation for the claims Jesus made about himself—that He predated Abraham and was therefore greater than the very father of the Jewish nation,[56] greater than its greatest king,[57] that he was not only the Son of God[58] but God the Son,[59] and with it, other issues that relate directly to the world we live in. Lots of claims we might have once dismissed now have to be examined, and one of those is Jesus' view of natural history. This is going to feel like a stretch—it's going to feel weird—but stay with me for a moment.

"One of the major problems with the free-will theodicy, and why it's fallen out of favor in modern times, is that it seemed to fly in the face of so much of what science was telling us. Mankind wasn't created in a state of innocence, which then fell by being disobedient to some command. Mankind was the end result of millions of years of evolutionary trial and error. Again, two wildly disparate pictures."

"So, like you said," Ray responded, "we need to see the Garden of Eden as in some way profoundly historical."

"For this theodicy to make sense, yes."

"That *is* going to be a mind-stretching idea."

"Maybe," Mike said, "but let me give you something that might help you build a conceptual bridge. Carl and I call this the two-timeframe theory."

"A two-timeframe theory?" Ray mused.

---

56   John 8:58.
57   Matthew 12:42, Luke 11:31.
58   Matthew 26:64, Mark 14:62, Luke 23:70, John 3:16, 18.
59   John 14:9, Matthew 28:19.

Mike nodded. "Consider Jesus' first miracle recorded in the Gospel according to John. Do you know what he did?"

Ray was quiet, not being sure. Libby filled in the gap. "He changed water to wine."

"*Instantly*," Mike added. "If you head up Interstate 26 through South Carolina, just as you get to the North Carolina state line, you'll enter an area that makes some great wine. The winemakers know how to do this and do it well. And it takes a lot of work, and it takes a lot of time—time to grow the grapes, time to harvest and juice them, time to age the juice in casks and then to bottle it. Jesus took six water pots containing about a hundred and fifty gallons of water and either compressed or compacted or removed time altogether and *instantly* created wine."

"You really believe he did this?" Ray asked.

"If he rose from the dead, Ray, then why not? Which is the bigger miracle?"

Ray thought about that for a moment then nodded.

"The point," Mike continued, "about any miracle is that time seems to be dispensed with or altered in nearly every case.

"Jesus healed a blind man in the ninth chapter of the same Gospel. The guy was more than forty years old. He'd been born blind. And now he could see. It got him in a bit of a pickle when it came to the attention of the authorities. But the question is, how old were his eyes once healed? How old were the once defective but now fixed parts? Forty years old? Minutes or hours old? Two timeframes—physiological and created—and, interestingly, both would be right.

"If we'd taken some of the wine from that wedding in Cana to a biochemist who was also an expert in wines, he might have been able to tell us the kind of grape, whether he thought the season it was grown in was dry or wet. He might also give us an educated guess as to its vintage—how old it was. And everyone who was anyone who knew anything about wine might have agreed with his guesstimate. Everyone, that is, except the guys who filled the stone water pots. Was it years old or hours?

"If we read about man's origin in Genesis, we find that Adam is made as a mature man. Instantly. Physiologically he was perhaps in his twenties. But from the standpoint of true time, he was only minutes or hours old. Two timeframes. Again, both would be right."

"So," Todd said, "am I hearing you correctly? You guys think the world is six thousand years old?"

"Are you even listening, Todd?" Libby said, with a hint of exasperation. "What he's saying is that we can be very comfortable with the idea that the world is four and a half billion years old."

"Or that the universe is nearly fourteen billion years[60] old," Eric added. "We're dealing with two timeframes."

"Chronological and created," Mike summarized. "For something to have the characteristics or structure it has—be that wine or the universe—under natural circumstances, it takes lots of chronological time to develop. But God is able to create with that developmental time frame already imbedded."

"And you don't think that makes God some kind of grand deceiver?" Ray asked.

"Why would that be?" Mike answered. "One of the fundamental characteristics of wine is that it is *aged*, fermented grape juice. If it's not aged and fermented, it's not wine; there's no other way to do it. In the wine he created, every molecule matched every other

---

60   The generally accepted age of the universe is 13.72 billion years old.

molecule from the standpoint of chronological time, or it wouldn't have been what it was. Whatever the blind man's eyes were, from the standpoint of the miracle or physiologically, they were functioning eyes for a forty-year-old man. It's the nature of the miraculous…if it ends up as part of the physical creation."

"But then," Ray interjected, "we'd never be able to distinguish between what developed naturally and what miraculously popped into existence."

"No. You could," Mike replied thoughtfully. "There would be clues."

"Clues?" Todd scoffed incredulously.

Mike shrugged. "The universe had a beginning. Things that begin to exist have causes. The universe is temporal, finite and material. This would mean (unless there is some universe-making machine out there, which would also need to be explained), the cause of this universe would have to be timeless, infinite and immaterial. Those are basic characteristics of God.

"We're not dealing with a Big Bang," Mike added, "in the way we'd think. The universe isn't the aftermath of some chaotic explosion. The cosmological constant—the universe's expansion rate—is fine tuned to 1:10 followed by fifty-three zeros. Change that number even slightly, and the early universe either expands too quickly for matter to coalesce—no galaxies, stars or planets, so no us—or it falls back in on itself in a big crunch."

"But this isn't proof, Mike," Todd said.

"No, not proof—clues," Mike reiterated. "The four fundamental constants in physics—the strong nuclear force, electromagnetism, the weak nuclear force and gravity—are balanced in relation to each other to an insane degree. Make the force of any one of them stronger or weaker in the least and you wipe out the universe, or make it unlivable. This place is finely structured—finely tuned.

"Our solar system exists in the only kind of galaxy it can be in where it won't get fried. We're in just the right spot to build a planet like ours—far enough in to have the building materials needed to make a terrestrial, earthlike planet, but far enough out to stay out of the way of exploding supernova, the gamma ray bursts and the black hole in the galactic center. We're nestled between galactic arms as well, so we're clear of a lot of the same stuff that goes on in them. We're in just the right spot in our *solar system* to have water. We have a nearly circular orbit around a star that varies in its nuclear output by one tenth of one percent—extraordinarily stable. The size of our moon that stabilizes our tilt, the composition of our atmosphere…. The fortuitous list for life goes on and on and on!

"Speculation runs rampant in an effort to explain how life mindlessly began, but origin of life research invariably gets stopped; no one has any real idea *how* it happened. Why? Because life itself is based on an informational hard drive, the genome, and meaningful information—information used in communication—like you just conceded, Ray, is inherently the product of conscious activity. And we have solid, historical evidence that Jesus rose from the dead. *Lots of converging clues—lots of converging lines of evidence.*

"Now consider this: Jesus made the comment when dealing with divorce that 'in the beginning, God made them male and female.'[61] *'In the beginning'* God created two sentient creatures with full gender development, not four and a half billion years after the fact. If Christ rose from the dead proving His divinity, and if evolutionary theory isn't the theory of everything we once thought it was, then we might

---

61   Matthew 19:4, Mark 10:6.

consider that Jesus knew what He was talking about; He would have been an eyewitness."

Ray smiled at the problems that would surface if that were the case. "Mike, if mankind was the first on the scene, then what do you do with things like dinosaurs?"

Dinosaurs, Mike thought. Was this something he wanted to get into? He realized he'd at least have to touch on it, or they couldn't move on. "Well, they've found organic matter—soft tissue, what is believed to be red blood cells and medullary bone, the calcium deposits inside leg bones used to build shell—in the femur of a supposed sixty-eight-million-year-old female, pregnant T-Rex,"[62] Mike answered.

"But," Ray rejoined, "the formation in Montana where that femur was found is known to be sixty-eight million years old!"

"You're right, Ray. And we also know this kind of soft tissue doesn't last for sixty-eight million years. So which assumptions do we toss and which assumptions do we stick with—our dating models or our experience with biological degeneration and fossilization?"

Ray said, "But they've now found that iron might have a lot to do with why that organic matter was preserved."[63]

Mike shook his head. "I read the same article. And there is a world of difference between preserving something for two years in a lab and sixty-eight million years in the wild. Is this another extravagant Darwinian extrapolation? We'll see. Certainly, a lot more work needs to be done."

---

62 http://www.smithsonianmag.com/science-nature/dinosaur.html?c=y&page=1.
   http://www.science20.com/curiousity_killed_fruit_fly/bones_contention_
   dinosaur_cells_survived_millions_years_trapped_bone-95449.
63 http://www.livescience.com/41537-t-rex-soft-tissue.html
   See Appendix II—The Question of Dinosaurs

Ray shrugged and nodded a quiet agreement, and then Mike added, "You know, Todd wanted to talk about whale evolution the other day, but we didn't go there because we didn't have time. That's a conversation that can and did take place somewhere else. The resurrection is something that would be helpful to unpack too, for Todd's sake, but it's a major conversation, and for now we don't have the time. And I'm going to suggest that the dinosaurs are the same thing.

"I'm not dodging this," Mike continued. "I hope you've seen by now that I don't shy away from the hard questions; we handle them pretty much head on. I'm just afraid the subject will take us too far afield, and we still have some ground to cover. I'll be happy to take up the subject later, but you do need to know, at the end of the day, the dinosaurs wouldn't make a whit of difference one way or the other."

"Really," Todd said. He didn't sound at all convinced.

"I promise," Mike said assuredly.

Ray smiled quietly. "I'll let it go for now, Mike. I don't know how the dinosaurs couldn't be a big deal, but I've been surprised by your handling of things before. You *have* shown me that you do face things straight on. So we'll let it go for now."

Mike smiled. "I appreciate the vote of confidence. I'll do my best to make sure it's well placed."

Mike took a deep breath. "Okay," he added, "we're rounding third base heading for home." He then smiled sheepishly. "Sorry. Guy analogy again....unless you're playing girls' softball."

Both girls chuckled; they knew what he meant even though neither played the sport.

Chapter Seven

Connecting the Dots

"To move toward an answer to your second question, Ray—why God may seem so indifferent to the chaos and destruction and what it does to his creation—we need to see we are ultimately dealing with the idea of immortality, that mankind can and will live forever in some future state. And here's the question: Will we be more free or less free then?"

Libby chimed in as if reciting a dream. "I've always thought of heaven as being better, brighter, more of everything—more colors, more fragrances, more beauty. Clearer days, clearer vision. Everything we have here, just more of it, and better. So," she said laughingly, "I guess I'd have to say *more* free!"

Eric nodded his enthusiastic agreement as did Chelsea. Todd remained quiet, watching. But Ray said, "For the sake of argument, I'm with Libby."

"Okay," Mike said. "So here's another problem, and it has to do with the angels."

"The angels." Ray chuckled, shaking his head.

"I know." Mike smiled. "Another idea for the modern, scientific mind to grapple with…you know, to go with the two timeframes, the garden and innocent humans falling into sin." Mike waited for the psychological angst to play out then asked, "Shall I continue?"

Ray nodded, as did Todd. They wanted to see where this argument would end up.

"The angels lived in heaven with God supposedly before creation. They saw him face to face; they had complete access to him. Yet they fell.[64] Theologians and philosophers have wondered how this happened and how their experience might apply to us in our future state. Being immortal and being in such close proximity to God, for them there was no righting the ship once it had gone wrong; they were *done*. If we are truly free, then what's to keep us from following that same rebellious course of action in our immortal future?"

The siblings looked at each other, surprised. "I'd never thought about that, Mike," Libby admitted.

Todd said nothing, but Ray said, "I'm waiting."

"Scholars have speculated about this," Mike continued, "and one idea is that, in our immortal future, God will give mankind the inability to sin."[65]

---

64 See Appendix III—The Fall of the Angels.

65 *Non Posse Peccare*—a concept introduced by Augustine of Hippo where the fourfold nature of human will, with regard to sin, is delineated. Before the fall we

"The inability to sin?" Ray smiled. "The inability to fail in some moral way? Then you're not freer in your future state, Mike. What's the difference between being given an inability and removing an ability? Either way your freedom is impacted—compromised—so much so that it might be argued you are no longer free at all. It seems like a fancy, philosophical shell game to me."

"Initially that was Carl's and my assessment too," Mike admitted. "From a practical standpoint, if God could give us an inability to sin, then why didn't he do it in the garden before the fall and avoid all this mayhem and destruction that ultimately resulted in the death of his own Son?"

Mike stopped for a moment once more to allow the mental dust to settle and perhaps allow an intellectual tension to build too.

"So what's the solution, Big Guy?" Todd finally asked.

Mike took a sip of coffee. "The thinking behind this 'giving us an inability' is, again, that we only do what we are inclined to do and that in heaven God would somehow remove our inclination to sin. In effect, that God will remove our *desire* to sin."

"Same diff, Mike," Ray asserted. "You're still messing with our volitional nature—the essence of what makes us human. The rabbis have always taught that doing that put the kibosh on the whole deal; it was something God would never do. Freedom is too essential

---

had the ability to sin and the ability not to sin—*Posse Peccare, Posse Non Peccare.* After the fall we find we have the ability to sin and the inability not to sin—*Non Posse Non Peccare* (further discussed by Paul in Romans, chapter 7). Once we come to Christ we regain the ability not to sin, but we retain the ability to sin—*Posse Peccare, Posse Non Peccare.* But once in heaven, in eternity, we have the ability not to sin and are given the inability to sin—*Posse Peccare, Non Posse Peccare.* To some, this is a theology of great comfort; we will never fail in the future. To others, it appears to be a "bridge too far" because it appears to violate the very core of human nature—our free will. The argument *for* the position is again that we only do what we are inclined to do and that when we enter heaven all of our inclinations to sin will be removed.

to the whole picture. *Free* to succeed means we're *free* to fail. *Free* to love means we're *free* not to. *Free* to doubt means we're *free* to believe. It's what makes any of these things mean anything at all. If you remove one of the choices, you remove them both; they go hand in hand."

Mike nodded. "Okay. Let me take a different swing at this. Let's step back for a moment to make sure the ground we're covering is properly understood. And one question we might need to ask is, what's the difference between us and the angels? That might have a bearing on how mankind's future decisions may well differ from the angels' past ones. I *will* tell you, not much is known about them.

"We can surmise that we are the same with the angels in the fact that we are both *created*, *contingent* [66] creatures. Some have speculated that angels are not truly free, but the New Testament tells us we will one day judge them [67] and that God will judge them too, [68] and how do you judge something that isn't culpable?"

"It makes no sense," Ray said.

"No, it doesn't," Mike added. "So it can be agreed that angels and man are both rational and free. [69] One might wonder then about what was going on before the angels fell. Did God counsel them about evil? Remember, theoretical evil has been a dormant option as long as God has been holy—from the get-go. Was there a fatherly conversation in heaven with His archangels in the same way he

---

66   Contingent as opposed to necessary. A necessary being (God) *must* exist; he has no cause—no antecedent. A contingent being (angelic or human) depends on something or someone else for its existence.

67   1 Corinthians 6:3.

68   2 Peter 2:4, Revelation 12:9.

69   When we look at the different interpersonal actions of these beings—the serpent in the garden (Genesis 3:1-7), the accuser in Job (Job 1:6-11, 2:1-5), Gabriel with Daniel (Daniel 8:17, 9:22-27), and later with Zacharias (Luke 1:13-17, 19-20) and Mary (Luke 1:26-37), they all appear fully rational.

counseled Cain before Abel was murdered?[70] Did God warn them about this—that if someone got the feeling they were bumping up against some kind of glass ceiling[71] and wanted to take matters into their own hands, that the consequences would be catastrophic[72] and apparently irreversible?"

Eric stopped him. "You said they were done before, and you're now claiming that what the angels did was irreversible."

"Yes." Mike nodded. "No recourse to undo what had been done. The author of the letter to the Hebrews speaks to this." At this, Mike found the quote on his tablet: "'For assuredly He does not give help to angels, but He gives help to the descendants of Abraham.'"[73]

"And why's that?" Todd asked.

"They were *immortal* when they fell."

"So what difference does that make?"

"That's a good question," Mike replied. "The answer goes to the heart of what we're talking about, and we'll address it, but I need to build a case first. Let me insert one other thing here that will bring the answer into view. I want to put together a picture of the fall of man from the viewpoint of an atheist—my brother."

"Your brother's an atheist, Mike?" Libby asked not a little surprised.

Mike smiled. "It's understandably one of the driving forces in my life behind my insatiable appetite for apologetics.

"Anyway, my brother shared with me his take on Genesis one day, and it was very astute. He said, 'Okay, so God makes Adam and Eve and puts them in this garden. Let's agree they are a little wet

---

70   Genesis 4:7.
71   Isaiah 14:13-14.
72   Isaiah 14:12, 15.
73   Hebrews 2:16.

behind the ears—not a lot of street smarts; they hadn't been around long enough to pick that up. So God points out this tree—the tree of the knowledge of good and evil—which makes it something of considerable interest. Then he announces the prohibition. And then he leaves. Anyone even remotely familiar with child psychology would know that's a recipe for disaster.'"

Ray and Todd both smiled and nodded in agreement. Eric and Libby didn't quite know what to think, nor did Chelsea.

Then Mike continued. "I had to admit, the observation was unsettling. James, Jesus' half-brother, wrote an epistle where he claimed that God never tempts anyone.[74] Teenagers I work with have asked what the difference is between a temptation and a test. They sure feel like the same thing. My answer has always been that they *are* the same thing. The circumstances don't differ one bit. Just read the opening chapters of Job. The difference, I tell them, has to do with the motivations of the one behind the circumstances. God tests us to prove us. Satan tempts us to seduce us.[75] God wants us to pass the test, to show our mettle, to grow. Satan wants us to fail and eventually be destroyed by all the small choices—the compromises, the constantly giving in. But my brother's take on the situation in the garden seemed to cross that threshold.

"I shared his view on Genesis with Carl, and he admitted the point was well made. Then he added something even more troubling—that when God left, he knew he was leaving us in the company of someone with the wiles to use our new knowledge against us. If God knows everything, then he knew the serpent was

---

74   James 1:13.
75   "The Devil tempts that he may ruin and destroy. God tests that He may crown." Ambrose, Bishop of Milan (340-397).

there. Carl and I couldn't figure this out—God wanted us to fail? And that failure eventually resulted in the torture and execution of his Son? It made no sense!

"We went round and round about this for a week. We knew there must be an answer, but what was it? Anyway, I'm at church picking up Carl for lunch, and he's stuck in a meeting with the senior pastor, and my wife calls while I'm waiting. She tells me the air conditioning repairman is going to be at our house at three o'clock and asks if I can be there. I told her no problem, but I ask her where she's going to be. She said at the doctor's getting our kids their shots. We have four.

"Our eight-year-old—Brooke—was at Ray's daughter's first birthday party." Then he shook his head in Ray's direction. "It seems like just yesterday...."

Ray nodded soberly.

Mike took a deep breath. "The other three are five, three and eighteen months. Unlike a lot of parents, my wife's honest with our kids. When they are old enough, she tells them, 'We're going to the doctor today, and you're going to get a shot, and it's going to hurt; but it's going to protect you from something that would hurt you far worse. And Mommy's going to be with you, and it's going to be okay. And then we'll go get some ice cream.' This is a real relief to the nurses who give them their shots. Our kids don't freak out when brought in for these things; they're prepared, at least the older ones. But the three-year-old and eighteen-month-old are a different matter. They still look up at Mommy with those wide, tear-filled, saucer eyes that plead, 'Mommy, why are you letting this big person stick me with the big thing that hurts me?! Don't you love me??!!'

"I got off the phone shaking my head; vaccinations are the bane of every loving parent. And then it hit me. *We're involved in a giant inoculation project…!*"

"Not following you, Mike," Ray said.

"How does God remove our desire to sin without actually touching the core of what makes us human—our free will? The only way to do it is to create a controlled situation where we'd experience the consequences of rebellion, where evil is unleashed—the fear and alienation, the violence and inequities, disease, famine, war, suffering and death—and where we take it in the teeth until it's coming out our ears and nostrils. And then begin again."

Libby looked concerned. "But, Mike, this would mean that God meant for us to fail."

Mike nodded. "In the same way our pediatrician wants my kids to get exposed to the measles, the mumps and rubella—in a *controlled* way through the vaccines."

"But those aren't moral failures, Mike," Eric now said. "You're saying God set us up for moral failure. That makes God culpable."

Mike shook his head. "God didn't make the decision, Eric; we did. All he did was allow for the inevitable to be accelerated so as to control it. Let me show this to you in a little different way.

"Jacques Maritain said, and I'll paraphrase, 'If something can happen, it will happen eventually.'[76] And he's right; we all know this. Look—Ray and I both own our homes. The chances that his house or mine will catch fire and burn down is remote. But the chance that a house somewhere in the state of Florida is going to catch fire and burn down is high. And when we make that control

---

76   Jacques Maritain, *The Problem of Evil*, Milwaukee, WI, Marquette University Press, 1942, p. 6.

group the whole country the chance moves to the level of certainty. Insurance companies can chart these losses using their actuarial tables almost with the precision of the movement of the planets. It's called the law of large numbers. As you move from smaller to larger control groups, you make the plausible possible, then probable and then a certainty."

Ray's eyes got bright. "That sounds like a great argument *for* Darwinism, my intelligent design comrade."

"For Darwinism to work, Ray, *first you need a house*. Then the certainty would have to be inserted at the level of implausible; we'd need fifty of them a day burning down in *Gainesville*."

Ray just chuckled and shook his head. It was just one of many times they saw the glass half full/half empty equation differently. But knowing they were dealing with an entirely different subject, Ray kindly let it go.

"But back to the idea of inoculation," Mike said. "Knowing well the lethal combination of theoretical evil and a rational, free creature, and that the exercise of the option was inevitable, why wait? Why wait for kids to be in the picture—humans going here and there, eating from this tree and that one? Why deal with the inevitable failure multiple times in multiple ways? Why not allow for the fall to happen one time from the get-go—lump human moral failure all together from the outset through Mom and Dad and allow mankind to experience the horrors of what they'd chosen as a single group? And then, when it was time, write the check once and for all to pay for the whole shootin' match."

Eric and Libby looked thoughtful. They didn't like things being orchestrated in this way, but what Mike was saying made sense.

Todd wasn't having any problems with Mike's rationales; defending God's character wasn't an issue for him. Besides, Mike's positions had all seemed weird to him. But he was following the argumentation. "You sound like God's a risk manager. You even said he's going to do this like a controlled experiment, right? So what makes this controlled?"

"Mortality," Mike answered.

"Come again?" Ray asked.

"God sentenced us to mortality. He said, 'In the day you eat of it, you shall die.'"[77]

"But we didn't," Todd interjected.

"Not in the way you and I would think," Mike replied. "But in a real sense we did spiritually and began to physically. And it was a living death; we became dead to God—the very Author of our life. Paul talked about us being 'dead in our transgressions and sins.'[78] In the garden there was, in fact, an immediate concern that our living death might become a permanent condition."

"A permanent condition?" Eric asked.

"Remember," Mike said, "the Scriptures quote God as saying, 'Behold the man has become like one of Us, knowing good and evil, and now, he might stretch out his hand and take also from the tree of life and eat and live forever.'[79] He therefore took immediate action by driving us out of the garden and stationing the cherubim

---

77 Genesis 2:17.
78 Ephesians 2:1.
79 Genesis 3:22 (Note: Many believe the plural form 'Us' used in this verse, as in 1:26, is an allusion to the triune nature of God—one God in three Persons. This is a reasonable position though not universally accepted. The case is also made that it is God speaking to the hosts of heaven. The two passages do deal with the act of creation and with the knowledge of good and evil. Whether or not these can be as easily applied to the hosts of heaven as they are to God is something to consider.)

to 'guard the way to the tree of life.'[80] If you read this passage, it becomes clear that God wasn't concerned about the garden anymore, nor was he concerned about protecting the tree of life from us. He was concerned about protecting us from the tree of life. Why?

"If we'd eaten from it and become immortal while fallen—a living death forever—God's option to save us would have vaporized. You see, our sentence of death was not only our judgment; it was also our means of escape.

"You asked before, Todd, why God doesn't give help to the angels. It appears it's because he can't. The angels were immortal when they fell. There was apparently no legal way for him to undo what had been done. Mankind was different. By sentencing us to mortality when we fell, it put us in a finite box where the damage could be limited and experienced, but where it could also be undone."

"Undone?" Todd asked.

Mike nodded. "The apostle Paul told us, 'The wages of sin is death.'[81] Ray knows this; the Jewish sacrificial system was based on it.[82] By God making us mortal, he gave himself the very tools and strategy to extricate us from our predicament. It allowed his Son to eventually enter into our finite humanness—that incarnation idea we talked about last week, Todd. By that, he could take on our humanity and our sentence and die our death for us. Without being sentenced to mortality, he wouldn't have had this available. Again our sentence was not only our judgment, but it also became our way out."

---

80 Genesis 3:24.
81 Romans 3:23.
82 Leviticus 17:11, Hebrews 9:22.

Ray began shaking his head. "There's one problem with this grand story of yours, Mike, and that's the same problem we find with your soul-building idea. Even if I could rewrite my entire understanding of natural history and accept your two-timeframe theory—that puts Adam and Eve *in the beginning* in this innocent state from which they fell—it doesn't answer the horrendous problem of natural evil. The biosphere around us is in a world of hurt, and these creatures suffer, and they had nothing to do with Adam and Eve's stupidity, inevitable though it may have been."

Mike nodded, but he was ready. "Follow me for a moment. Let me take you back to Southampton, England, on April 10, 1912. We're standing on the dock watching the world's largest moving object cast off. We see the family and friends of the Titanic's passengers waving but then turn around and see a platform. And we recognize that on that platform are the members of the White Star Line's board of directors. And they're all looking up at a solitary figure on the bridge, Edward Smith, the most experienced and trusted sea captain on the North Atlantic. He'd been doing this for forty years.

"They know, as the Titanic pulls away, that their authority, as it pertains to this ship and this voyage inexorably passes to Captain Smith. Their dreams and vision for the Titanic rest on his shoulders. Once at sea, he *was* the White Star Line. If he decided to be aggressive or reckless in trying to set a transatlantic record, or if he chose to be prudent, to be cautious with their investment, the fate of the company, and the fate of all those who'd put their lives in the company's hands, would be directly affected by *his* decisions alone—no one else's. And the rest is history.

"On the night of April 14th, in spite of warnings about the ice, in spite of running in a dead calm which meant no waves would be breaking on the base of the icebergs allowing them to be seen, in spite of no moon to allow his lookouts to see far enough ahead, Smith gave the order to maintain course and speed—twenty-two knots. And more than fifteen hundred people *who had nothing to do with his decision*—no input or say-so at all—died…in a terrifying way.

"The apostle Paul talked about this very thing. Remember, Genesis records that Adam named the animals. Why? Because he had been given *full dominion*—dominion over the 'the fish of the sea, and the birds of the sky, and over the cattle and every creeping thing…'[83] He was made captain of the ship. Paul said, in his letter to the Romans—here, let me read it." Mike pulled up the passage on his tablet and began to read:

> For the anxious longing of this creation waits eagerly for the revealing of the sons of God (that's you and me). For the creation was subjected to futility, not willingly, but because of Him who subjected it, in hope that the creation itself also will be set free from its slavery to corruption into the freedom of the glory of the children of God (*our* glory, not God's). For we know that the whole of creation groans and suffers the pains of childbirth until now.[84]

"Paul's associate, Luke, records in his Gospel that when Jesus made his triumphant entry into Jerusalem, and everyone was singing his praises, the Pharisees told Christ to rebuke them. And he replied,

---

83 Genesis 1:26.
84 Romans 8:19-22 (parentheses mine).

'If these become silent, the stones will cry out.'[85] There's stuff going on in nature—an expectancy—we know nothing about."

Ray rejoined dryly, "And yet the creatures continue to kill and eat each other. Was this God's plan?"

"How long has it been since you've read Genesis, Ray? All creatures including man were given 'every *plant* yielding seed... and every *tree* that has fruit yielding seed...shall be food for you and every beast of the earth...and every bird of the sky....'[86] Everything was originally herbivorous. That's the way it was before the fall, at least.

"And Isaiah tells us that's the way it will end up. 'The wolf and the lamb will graze together, and the lion will eat straw like the ox.... They will do no evil or harm on all My holy mountain, says the Lord.'[87] It's the way He's always intended it to be."

This all seemed like such a stretch for Ray, but he allowed Mike's commentary. He wanted to get to the bottom of the argument. "So let me see if I can pull all this together. You're saying the garden was a setup."

"If you want to use that terminology," Mike said. "Again, all God did was allow for Adam and Eve's inevitable decision to be compressed into a controlled timeframe and set of circumstances. One race, one fall, one payment."

Mike added, "In his letter to a church in Greece, Paul talks about Christ in two ways—as the *last* Adam and the *second* man.[88] As the last Adam, he'd be bringing up the rear; he's the consummation of the first race of man. Jesus mentioned that if he was lifted up he

---

85   Luke 19:40.
86   Genesis 1:29-30.
87   Isaiah 65:25.
88   1 Corinthians 15:45-47.

would draw all mankind to himself.[89] He would take us all to the cross and end things there.[90] And then, on Easter morning, as the second man, we'd begin again."[91]

"And if you're right," Ray continued, "then at least part of this equation is so that we can have a full-blown experience with the consequences of our stupidity—our rebellion—have it come out of our ears and nostrils, as you so aptly described it, so that our desire to sin would be expunged."

Mike shrugged. "Once burned, twice shy. You put your hand on the hot frying pan once, will you ever have the desire to do it again?"

"So just from the standpoint of experience," Ray summarized, "we'd have our *desire* to sin removed, which allows for its eradication, without touching or compromising our innate freedom." Ray's eyes narrowed as the conclusion sank in. "Pretty slick."

Mike stayed quiet, listening intently, waiting for Ray to continue the summary.

Libby then asked, "So how does this help you answer your second question, Ray?"

Ray grew thoughtful but began to nod as the realization hit home. "The reason God seems to sit so idly by as evil and suffering ravage what he's made is because the more horrendous our experience with it—"

"The more indelible the lesson," Mike finished his thought.

"Wow." Ray shook his head quietly. "It all fits. And the thing that makes all this work is that once we learn it, we don't just

89   John 12:32.
90   Romans 6:6, Galatians 2:20.
91   2 Corinthians 5:17.

disappear into oblivion; we get to start over again. Our encounter with evil is purposeful; it's a lesson we can carry forward."

"In two ways," Mike added. "Again, if God is going to work something deep into us from the standpoint of character—that soul-building we discussed—he would do it here and now, during our mortal existence. But the idea of inoculation would also be every bit a driving rationale.

"The Scriptures tell us that when we get to heaven, God will wipe away every tear from our eyes,[92] but it says nothing about his erasing our memories. We might find that our experience with evil is one of the fundamental assets of heaven."[93]

Todd began to shake his head. "If heaven is real, Mike, you can't have it both ways. I mean, how in the world can God wipe away every tear from our eyes *without* erasing our memories? You know my story. I have some memories I wouldn't want to follow me there, if I were to go. And as bad as my experiences have been, I'm sure they're a Sunday school picnic compared to others—people who've been brutalized or murdered, women who've been raped or watched their children die of starvation. In fact, I'd guess everyone would have memories they wouldn't want to carry through the pearly gates—either things they did or things that happened to them, if you get my drift."

Mike's expression showed he understood. Then he offered, "I get your point, Todd. There *are* personal experiences that might

---

92   Revelation 21:4.
93   Isaiah 65:17 says: "For behold, I create new heavens and a new earth; And the former things shall not be remembered or come to mind." An unequivocally literal interpretation of this text would render our mortal existence meaningless. This might be better understood in a general, rhetorical sense, not unlike some of Jesus' comments (Matthew 18:8–9, Mark 9:43–47, Luke 14:26). A more reasonable understanding is what Mike gives Todd in response to his following objection.

need to be forgotten if God is indeed to wipe away *every* tear. Or perhaps God wraps them in a cloak of his love and grace and even gives us a chance to see his allowed purposes in those experiences. We would then know the truth, and the truth would set us free, and one of those effects, I'm sure, would be to mitigate the pain going forward.

"But what I'm really talking about is the bigger picture—our corporate experience with the consequences of our choice to disobey him—what that meant to our lives as a whole. Think of it as waking up from a bad dream. We might not remember the particulars; we just know we don't want to go back into the nightmare. And the reason we were there in the first place is because we'd decided to commit, as the judge pointed out last week, cosmic treason. I think the ultimate effect will be to remove that choice from any and all future consideration."

Ray then added, "I'd agree with you, Todd, but when hearing Mike describe this, I'm also thinking in terms of the bigger picture. And the cool thing is that we get to go there. If Mike is right, and his point is beginning to make sense, by God sentencing us to 'death'—mortality—it allowed Jesus, the Messiah, to enter into our finiteness, our humanness, take on our sentence and die our death for us."

Mike replied, "That's what Isaiah meant when he said, 'He laid on him the iniquity of us all.'[94] And Paul said as much: 'He made him who knew no sin to become sin for us, that we might become the righteousness of God in him.'"[95]

"That's a remarkable trade," Ray said thoughtfully.

---

94   Isaiah 53:6.
95   2 Corinthians 5:21.

Todd shook his head again. "But that's the thing that blows this whole mind-numbing story for me. Even if I could get past the idea of no evolution, of the two timeframes, Adam and Eve being innocent and all, to me, the crucifixion is one of the most ridiculous ideas there is. God's not loving if he requires that of his own kid. Why not just forgive us? What loving father allows anything even closely resembling that to happen to his own child? Besides, it's not justice if someone else pays my tab. It's just nuts!"

"Why *not* just forgive us?" Mike repeated. "Would the judge be a good jurist if he'd just forgiven Chelsea? She's a good girl—she's on the dean's list—so why not? What about justice?"

Todd was quiet, but Ray looked at Mike and said, "You stopped me in my tracks last May when you went through that infinite-finite thing. You remember what you said?"

Mike nodded he did. In fact, it was right where he was going. "Todd, God is not only the Creator of this universe, and the great lover of his creation, but he's also its Chief Justice. And this means he has an uncompromising position with uncompromising responsibilities. So, with that in mind, let me lay out a scenario for you.

"If I shoplift a candy bar from the front counter here and get caught, that carries a certain consequence. If I pull out a gun and hold up the cashier and get caught, that's a different consequence altogether. In each case, the punishment fits the crime. But…if I sin against the infinite holiness of an infinite Being, something we've all done, the consequences to be just must be infinite. The problem is that you and I are finite. We can't experience infinite consequences in a finite period of time. We can only experience those infinite consequences in an infinite period of time. The Bible calls this eternal damnation. There is but one alternative to this, and that is if for us—for you and me—an infinite Being experiences those infinite consequences in a finite period of time. And this is what Christians call Good Friday."[96]

He paused then added, "Like I told Ray, Jesus had to be human[97] to pick up the tab, but he had to be divine[98] to pay it."

Todd peered at Mike with a surprised look on his face; he seemed dumbfounded. His eyes then dropped as he replayed Mike's explanation; he was working through a lot. Then slowly he nodded his head and said quietly, "Wow. I didn't see *that* coming."

Libby looked at her brother and smiled. Eric knew what she was thinking: he's not far from figuring this all out. But Chelsea thought she was seeing something else. She reached over, softly touched his hand and said, "Eric and Libby have told me how you lost your dad. You don't have to carry this, you know. You can let it go. It's not God's fault. You've been seeing him through the wrong lenses. He's good. He's given us everything he can. And he loves you. You need to give him the benefit of the doubt and see him through your own eyes, not the glasses given you at your dad's funeral."

Todd shook his head quietly. "That's not the whole story."

"No, it's not," Mike agreed seriously. "But the answer is. Every word of it."

They all watched now as a deep, emotional struggle worked its way to the surface. Todd's face became contorted as he fought back

---

96   See E. Calvin Beisner, *Answers for Atheists, Agnostics, and Other Thoughtful Skeptics: Dialogs about Christian Faith and Life,* Wheaton, IL, Crossway Books, 1993, p. 103.

97   Romans 8:3.

98   Colossians 1:19, 20.

tears, as the anger was seen for what it was—the product of a lie he'd carried for years. But what happened next made it all worth it.

Ray was watching Todd as he tried to compose himself. As he regained his emotional footing, Ray then looked back at Mike and said, "So…where do I sign?"

Seeing all that was happening in these two lives, the fruition of so much prayer, was something to behold. Mike smiled broadly at Ray, letting him know he was ready to help him take that next step. But before he did, he wanted to see if someone else wanted to join them. "Todd…?"

Where Do I Sign?

And so our story comes to an end, or does it?

You might wonder what Ray was asking Mike when he said, "Where do I sign?" He was asking Mike how he could become a Christian. This was no spur-of-the-moment decision. What brought him to this point?

The previous year, Eric had asked some penetrating questions in Ray's class, questions that opened up the subject of Darwinism, showing that a great many questions could be asked and that many of the current answers to them were insufficient. This gave Ray a reason to rethink his unquestioned allegiance to the theory and to the philosophy that leaves no real room or role for God.

Second, Mike had encouraged him to rethink Jesus as his Messiah. Mike had followed that up by giving Ray material dealing with the historical case for Christ's bodily resurrection from the dead, information Ray admitted was very compelling, and something that, if it were true, would change everything.

And now Mike had given him sufficient answers to the biggest challenge to his faith in God: the problem of evil. The way had been cleared for Ray to enter into that greatest and most meaningful of all relationships—a personal relationship with his loving Creator and Redeemer.

Did Todd come too? You can answer that. Todd was both honest enough to ask the big questions and courageous enough to follow the answers wherever they took him.

If you feel the reasons given here answer *your* questions, and you haven't done so, let me encourage you to do personal business with the God of the universe. It's simple. He loves you. He made you for himself. He knows you far better than you know yourself; he knows the number of hairs on your head.[99] He's given himself for you. Why not give yourself to him? You can do so by simply praying:

> God and Father, you made us for yourself, but we fell into sin and betrayed your love and trust. But you loved us and gave us your only Son, to live and die as one of us. Thank you. I receive what Christ did for me that horrible day— that "good" day above all others. Thank you that he paid the price for my sins. But you didn't stop there. You raised him from the dead. So now I cannot only be forgiven, but I can have a new life[100] in him too.
>
> Please apply what he did to me, forgive my sins and clothe me in his moral perfection, his righteousness. Receive me and make me your own. And let me live from

---

99   Matthew 10:30, Luke 12:7.
100   2 Corinthians 5:17.

this day on as your child. Come, Holy Spirit, and live in and through me, that I might know this new life in Christ. Amen.

If you've prayed this prayer, talk to a Christian friend, find a church and a pastor you can relate to—someone who can mentor you. And begin reading God's Word, the Bible…perhaps start with the Gospel of John. God bless you as you seek to grow in this newfound faith in Christ. As Christian music artist Steven Curtis Chapman describes it, your new relationship to Christ is "the great adventure"!

Clayton Brumby
John 1:12

Appendix I

Exposing a Darwinian Straw Man

Ray Cohen described Kenneth Miller's handling of an argument made for the irreducible complexity of the cilium by Michael Behe as a straw man—misrepresenting and then answering an argument not made by Behe. What follows is why, in the story, in spite of being a Darwinist, Ray came to this conclusion.

In 1996, Lehigh University biochemistry professor Michael Behe published his first book, *Darwin's Black Box*. In it he introduced the concept of irreducible complexity. Irreducible complexity simply claims certain structures or systems in biology show a *function* that is the result of the interworking or interdependence of a number of well-matched parts. Remove one of the parts, and the function is lost. Therefore it cannot be the product of step-by-step Darwinian processes (an interworking of chance and natural law). As Michael Behe says in his second book, *The Edge of Evolution*, "A common mechanical mousetrap is an example of irreducible complexity because it 'is composed of several well-matched, interacting parts that contribute to the basic *function*' and 'the removal of any one of the parts causes the system to effectively cease *functioning.*'" [101] In other words, the design is real. It required premeditation, coordination, seeing a goal, using reason; it required intelligence. And cilia are an example of this. Irreducible complexity is therefore a direct challenge to Darwinian evolution.

In his seminal book, *The Origin of Species,* Charles Darwin claimed his theory could be falsified by demonstrating that an irreducibly complex system existed.

> If it could be demonstrated that any complex organ existed which could not possibly have been formed by numerous, successive, slight modifications, my theory would absolutely break down.[102]

Michael Behe took Darwin up on his challenge and falsified his theory.

There's a small problem with this, of course. Currently, institutional science holds a privileged place in Western culture; it is the unquestioned authority on all things intellectual. And,

---

101 THE EDGE OF EVOLUTION by Michael J. Behe. Copy-right © 2007, by Michael J. Behe. Reprinted by per-mission of Simon & Schuster Publishing Group from the Free Press Edition. All rights reserved. p. 120 (em-phasis mine). Behe quotes from his first book, DAR-WIN'S BLACK BOX, by Michael J. Behe. Copyright © 1996, 2006 by Michael J. Behe. Reprinted by permis-sions of Simon & schuster Publishing Group from the Free Press Edition. All rights reserved. p. 39.

102 Charles Darwin, *The Origin of Species*, sixth edition, Oxford, Oxford University Press, 1998, p. 154.

as Ray put it, Darwinian Theory is currently "the central dogma of modern biology...." For Darwinists to be shown to have gotten such a fundamental question wrong is simply not going to fly. Scientists have staked their life's work and reputations on this theory, so this challenge is not going to be taken lying down; there is far too much at stake. Enter Kenneth Miller, science textbook author, cell biologist and biology professor at Brown University. Kenneth Miller is, currently, one of Darwinism's most visible and articulate apologists.

In 1999 Miller wrote a no-holds-barred response to Behe's work, a book titled *Finding Darwin's God*. In it he takes on many of the examples Behe set forth as irreducibly complex, giving them, he believed, adequate Darwinian explanations. There are more than a few problems with Miller's counterclaims, not the least of which is his handling of the cilium. What follows is a summary of Behe's original argument then Miller's response. And then we will find ourselves in Ray's classroom as Eric cross-examines Miller's rebuttal. During the process we'll discover why, at least with this example, Ray comes to the conclusion that Miller's counterargument is a straw man.

Behe's Argument

In Behe's words, "A cilium is a structure that, crudely put, looks like a hair and beats like a whip. If a cell is free to move about in liquid, the cilium moves the cell much as an oar moves a boat. If the cell is stuck in the middle of a sheet of other cells, the beating cilium moves liquid over the surface of the stationary cell."[103] Cilia

103 DARWIN'S BLACK BOX by Michael J. Behe. Copyright © 1996, 2006 by Michael J. Behe. Reprinted by permission of Simon & Schuster Publishing Group

do both jobs. Sperm, as individual cells, use cilia to move about, as in the first example, whereas the inner linings of our esophagus have cilia moving mucus out of our lungs as in the second. But no one understood the intricate construction of this hair-like structure until the invention of the electron microscope. Behe provides a clear description on pages 59-60 of *Darwin's Black Box.* [104]

It's always recommended that you read someone (in this case Behe) in their own words. However, to summarize, the cilium is made up of three interworking components: a grouping of microtubules—shafts that give it its structure—bound together by nexin linkers, so that it works as a single unit and then motorized by dynein proteins, so that it moves. Behe's example was of a 9+2 configuration of microtubules—nine doublets (two microtubules fused together) encircling two single microtubules.

In concluding his argument, Behe observes, "What components are needed for a cilium to work? Ciliary motion certainly requires microtubules; otherwise, there would be no strands to slide. Additionally, it requires a motor, or else the microtubules of the cilium would lie stiff and motionless. Furthermore, it requires linkers to tug on the neighboring strands, converting the sliding motion into a bending motion and preventing the structure from falling apart. All of these parts are required to perform one function: ciliary motion. Just as the mousetrap does not work unless all of its constituent parts are present, ciliary motion simply does not exist in the absence of microtubules, connectors and

104 In scientific vernacular, a "black box" is simply something that was too small for former scientists to investigate using the level of technology available to them. Today technology allows us to delve ever deeper into the organic world because of inventions like the electron microscope. One might wonder if Darwin would have proposed his theory at all if he'd had access to modern technology. Life at the level revealed by instruments like the electron microscope is mind-bogglingly intricate.

motors. Therefore we can conclude that the cilium is irreducibly complex—an enormous monkey wrench thrown into its presumed gradual, Darwinian evolution." [105]

Miller's Rebuttal

On page 140 of his book *Finding Darwin's God*, Kenneth Miller begins his rebuttal by saying, "Because textbooks say that the '9+2' structure is found in everything from single-celled algae to human sperm, a biochemist might easily have assumed that this particular pattern was the only one that worked, hence the conclusion of irreducible complexity." [106]

Miller goes on to say, "Comparative studies on a wide variety of organisms (as in figure 5.2) show that there are many ways to make a working cilium or flagellum without some of the parts that Behe seems to believe are essential." [107] He then begins to discuss other arrangements—a 9+7 configuration found in the sperm of the caddis fly *Polycentropus,* then mosquitoes in the genus *Culex* with a different configuration (9+1) where one of the two central microtubules is missing. He continues, in the notes for his figure 5.2, by discussing eel sperm from *Anguilla* that are missing both central microtubules. (In a later paper [108] Miller uses the eel sperm example again, but this time he adds that the outer dynein arms are missing along with the 'central spokes.') *Lecudina tuzetae*, a protozoan, is a 6+0. *Diplauxis hatti,* another protozoan, has a fully

105 DARWIN'S BLACK BOX by Michael J. Behe. Copyright © 1996, 2006 by Michael J. Behe. Reprinted by permission of Simon & Schuster Publishing Group from the Free Press edition. All rights reserved. p. 64, 65.

106 FINDING DARWIN'S GOD by KENNETH R. MILLER. Copyright © 1999 by Kenneth R. Miller. Reprinted by permission of HarperCollins Publishers, p. 140.

107 Ibid. p. 141.

108 http://www.millerandlevine.com/km/evol/design1/article.html.

functioning 3+0 configuration. And finally, a gall midget—a type of extremely small fly—provides us with an example that isn't radial at all, a freeform arrangement where microtubules are found throughout the cilium.

On page 143, Miller concludes: "In nature, we can find scores of cilia lacking one or more of the components supposedly essential to the function of the apparatus. It shouldn't be surprising that these novel structures do not all work exactly like the 9+2 arrangement. Nonetheless, they all do work, and each one is successful in its own way. These are sperm cells, after all, and the price for a gene that produces a defect in sperm function is instantaneous elimination from the next generation. What we actually see among cilia and flagella in nature is something entirely consistent with Darwin's call for numerous gradations from the simple to the complex. Once we have found a series of less complex, less intricate, differently organized flagella, the contention that this is an irreducibly complex structure has been successfully refuted."[109]

Eric's Cross-Examination

Miller's rebuttal to Behe's irreducibly complex cilium argument was one of the handouts that contributed to Libby's struggle, a struggle that precipitated Mike coming up with a plan not only to give Eric the other side of the story but also the tools to effectively expose the issues normally left untouched in Ray's class. His rationales have already been discussed, but what haven't been were Eric's ground rules in doing so.

---

109 FINDING DARWIN'S GOD by KENNETH R. MILLER. Copyright © 1999 by Kenneth R. Miller. Reprinted by permission of HarperCollins Publishers, p. 143.

Mike and Carl Dunning, Mike's compatriot and the associate pastor at his church, gave Eric a short set of suggested protocols—three guidelines. First, he was to see that Ray was not the enemy. Ray was to be treated with the utmost deference and respect. He was actually to be high on Eric's prayer list during his senior year. Second, Eric was to give advanced biology his best efforts—on every test and quiz, every lab and every paper. He was also to be fully engaged in the class throughout the year on all subjects and discussions, not just Darwin. In doing so, he would win the right to be heard when the time came. Third, to cross-examine the handouts and other issues involving evolution, he was only to do so by asking open-ended questions; assertions and/or pontificating were "illegal." This was designed to make sure Ray felt in complete control of the discussion. If Eric succeeded, Ray would feel comfortable enough to allow the questions to keep coming, and the cross-examination could continue.

One other thing Mike and Carl trained Eric to do was to give himself a chance to put his best foot forward. If some subject or argument came up in class that he wasn't quite prepared for, let it slide for the day; there was always tomorrow. Take that night and dive into it on his own, or with Mike or Carl's help, and then bring it up the next day when he felt prepared to address it. And that's what he chose to do with the cilium. What follows is Eric's cross-examination of the Miller handout.

Eric had raised his hand, and Ray acknowledged him. Eric then said, "Yesterday we discussed the cilium and how Kenneth

Miller showed that Michael Behe's argument didn't fly." Ray nodded, so Eric continued. "I got curious, so I checked out Dr. Behe's book from the library. I wanted to read his argument in his own words."

Ray smiled. "Good idea." Then he looked at the rest of the class. "Anyone else think to do this?" His question was met with an embarrassed silence and the shaking of heads. "This might be why Eric has one of the top GPAs in the class." Turning back to Eric, he said, "So what did you find?"

Eric shrugged. "It doesn't appear to me that Miller actually refuted Behe, unless I'm wrong. And I was wondering if we could spend a little more time on this."

Ray nodded an okay. He was gratified that a student had taken such ownership of a subject.

"I guess my first question about it," Eric continued, "has to do with Dr. Miller's comments in his conclusion." At this, Eric began to read from Ray's handout quoting Miller, "What we actually see among cilia and flagella in nature is something entirely consistent with Darwin's call for numerous gradations from the simple to the complex. Once we have found a series of less complex, less intricate, differently organized flagella, the contention that this is an irreducibly complex structure has been successfully refuted."[110] Eric looked up at Ray. "Is Dr. Miller saying here that these differently structured cilia represent a bona fide evolutionary series and are evidence of some kind of lineage and therefore descent with modification?"

"I think that's obvious," Ray replied assuredly.

110 FINDING DARWIN'S GOD by KENNETH R. MILLER. Copyright © 1999 by Kenneth R. Miller. Reprinted by permission of HarperCollins Publishers, p. 143.

Eric smiled to himself and shook his head. "How can that be? I mean, for that argument to work at all, wouldn't these more primitive examples—the 9+0 and the 9+1—be associated with the more primitive organisms?"

Ray was struck by the question and grew thoughtful. Maybe Eric was onto something. He shrugged and looked back at his student to continue.

"But that's not what we see," Eric said. "The 9+2 is the one associated with the *most primitive* organism—the single-celled algae. For sure, the 3+0 and the 6+0 are found in the protozoa, but the other 'simpler' forms—9+1 and the 9+0—are found in organisms way further down the supposed evolutionary timeline from the algae and way more complex. So why are the more primitive arrangements found in the more advanced life forms?"

Eric stopped for a moment but added, "And then the more complex 9+7 is found in a caddis fly. As humans, we have the 'simpler' 9+2—a V8 instead of a V12—but in every other sense we're a whole lot more complex than the fly. These configurations are all over the map. I'm sorry, but I don't see any discernible evolutionary lineage at all. I mean, how can these remotely be considered 'a series,' to use Dr. Miller's expression? Am I missing something here?"

Ray smiled thoughtfully at Eric's questions. "Good points."

Eric might have appreciated the compliment, but he was too absorbed in the subject to show it. "The other issue appears to be something…." Eric shrugged, seemingly not able to bring himself to say it.

"Something what?" Ray asked.

"I don't know," Eric admitted. "I don't understand this guy. Either a fully credentialed science educator misses Dr. Behe's point entirely, or…."

Ray recognized that Eric was trying to be diplomatic; he didn't want to be seen as questioning the motives of a tenured professor. But he also had something to say, so Ray encouraged him. "Go on, Eric. It's all right. Make your case."

Eric shrugged. "Or he builds a straw man. I mean, watch what he does." By this point, Eric had everyone's attention.

He took a deep breath. "Behe uses the 9+2 to build his argument. He never mentions these other arrangements. Maybe he didn't know about them. Maybe he did, and he didn't feel it mattered. But by not mentioning them, he left his position open to criticism. That's agreed."

While saying this he pulled out Behe's book and opened it to the page marked by a sticky note. "But Behe wraps up his argument by saying, 'What components are needed for a cilium to work? Ciliary motion certainly requires microtubules; otherwise, there would be no strands to slide. Additionally, it requires a motor, or else the microtubules of the cilium would lie stiff and motionless. Furthermore, it requires linkers to tug on the neighboring strands, converting the sliding motion into a bending motion, and preventing the structure from falling apart. All of these parts are required to perform one function: ciliary motion. Just as the mousetrap does not work unless all of its constituent parts are present, ciliary motion simply does not exist in the absence of microtubules, connectors and motors.'[111]

111 DARWIN'S BLACK BOX by Michael J. Behe. Copyright © 1996, 2006 by Michael J. Behe. Reprinted by permission of Simon & Schuster Publishing Group

"In other words, it seems that, contrary to Dr. Miller's assertions, Dr. Behe never marries himself to one particular arrangement of microtubules in cilia. He just said we need them, *and* the motor proteins, *and* the linkers—three things: *three* things that are essential for cilia *function*. But if we read Dr. Miller carefully, he never addresses those three things. All he argues about is the differing arrangements of one of them—the microtubules.

"So my question is this: Do these other arrangements of microtubules Dr. Miller points to have the nexin linkers? If they don't, can they be considered cilia? If I understand this correctly, an essential characteristic of cilia is that they are constructed of a grouping of microtubules—microtubules working together. And then, do they have the motor proteins—the little dynein guys? If they don't, again, are they cilia? Cilia move."

Another student in the class interjected, "But Miller showed that the eel sperm cilia lacked the outer dynein arms, didn't he?"

Ray nodded but kept quiet. He was intrigued by Eric's observations, and he wanted to stay out of the way; he wanted to see the students figure this out.

Eric replied, "But that just shows us that dynein proteins are present, doesn't it? Are these outer arms simply a feature, or are they essential? I mean, I can row a boat using two oars, or I can row a canoe using one.

"However the dynein proteins do it, they do it," Eric continued. "Eels keep reproducing which means the little outer-armless guys get 'er done. In fact, it appears that all of these different arrangements have the microtubules, the nexin linkers and the dynein proteins.

If Miller really wanted to refute Behe, wouldn't he have to show us cilia that lacked one of these three *truly essential* components and still worked?"

He stopped for a moment then added, "Wouldn't this be a classic straw man? You seemingly can't answer the argument made, so you construct one you can, sell it as the crux of the matter and then knock it down?"

Ray was mentally replaying Eric's comments. He then summarized, "So your assessment is that cilia *are* irreducibly complex after all?"

Eric nodded. "*All* the configurations are…it appears. Which means Dr. Behe's argument stands and Dr. Miller's refutation fails. Help me here. Where am I wrong?"

Ray grew quiet again as the full weight of Eric's observations began to sink in. Then he said, "I'm not at all sure you are."

And this was just the beginning. By the end of the unit on Darwin, Eric would approach every ancillary handout Ray gave the class in the same way.

It should be noted that, if Behe's argument for the irreducible complexity of the cilium stands, which it has so far, this also means that Darwinian Theory has been falsified using Darwin's own criterion. Other issues are currently emerging that only confirm this, and Ray admitted as much: The fact that the genome is a library of meaningful information, and meaningful information is an irrefutable marker of intelligence. That the genome itself is directed by another layer of information above it—the epigenome. That the gene expression system is itself irreducibly complex, being built of the very protein components it's supposed to build; so which came first? That there is virtually no discernible evolutionary development prior to the Cambrian boundary and that, beyond there, we have not been able to identify a single, *unimpeachable* transitional form *where one body plan becomes another*. So the irreducible complexity of the cilium is only the tip of the iceberg. It should be remembered, however—that's all it took to mortally wound the Titanic and send it to the bottom of the North Atlantic. Darwinists are drinking champagne and listening to the band on the upper decks, but the theory is down in the bow, and the lower decks are awash. It's only a matter of time.

Appendix II

The Question
of Dinosaurs

The same scientists named in the Smithsonian article have also found probable blood vessels and connective tissues in another T-Rex from Argentina and what appears to be the protein coat on a bird claw dated to some seventy to eighty million years ago, as well as the filament remains of a feather of a bird dating to the same period.[112] These living tissue remnants have been discovered because we stumbled upon them accidentally. According to paleontologist Thomas Holtz, Jr., at the University of Maryland, "The reason it hasn't been discovered before is no right-thinking paleontologist would do what Mary (Schweitzer) did with her (T-Rex) specimens. We don't go to all this effort to dig this stuff out of the ground to then destroy it in acid."[113]

---

112 http://www.nature.com/scientificamerican/journal/v303/n6/box/
       scientificamerican1210-62_BX2.html.
113 http://www.smithsonianmag.com/science-nature/dinosaur.html#ixzz2UbdNFYGf.

How much more of this type of material would be found among the millions of fossils we currently have in museums if they were tested in a similar way? No one saw the gargantuan flaw in the Hubble space telescope lens because it was so far out of the bounds of *what we were expecting* when doing the quality control checks prior to its deployment. It was only when we tried to use it to see deep into space that everyone saw what no one had been looking for or thought possible. It can be admitted that we have no paleontological or archeological finds showing humans were around dinosaurs—no footprints or tools. But the Scriptures tell us what might be a different story.

Job, chapter 40, tells us of behemoth whose tail was like a cedar tree trunk. That's not an elephant or a hippo, which have comparative flyswatters for tails. And then the author of Job talks about leviathan in chapter 41, as does the psalmist in Psalm 104.

The psalmist Asaph also tells us how God "crush(ed) the head of leviathan" and "gave him as food to the creatures of the wilderness (desert)."[114] There seems to be enough familiarity with this creature for it to be recognized both in the shipping lanes and in the desert, which is curious. How does a creature known for being aquatic end up in the desert wilderness? Yet that's exactly where Philip Gingerich found the remains of *Basilosaurus*—in the Zeuglodon valley, one hundred miles southwest of Cairo.[115] Is that where the psalmist saw the remains? Or someplace similar?

The comeback on this question is that dinosaurs *are* a big deal. T-Rex, for instance, was a dangerous creature. It would seem that

---

114 Psalm 74:14.
115 Stephen Jay Gould, "Hooking Leviathan by Its Past," *Natural History* 103 (May 1994): pp. 8-15. Philip D. Gingerich, "The Whales of Thethys," *Natural History* 103 (April 1994): pp. 86-88.

if they were in existence when mankind was around, there would be more mention of them in the most widely known of ancient texts—the Bible.

One possible explanation might be that when God created all the creatures of the biosphere, they filled the earth. And the earth is a big place. Mankind, though, was a very *localized* phenomenon. From the Scripture's testimony we are found, initially, only in the Near East. The great majority of the dinosaur population could have ranged far and wide and not been encountered by man. And other ancient documents outside of the Bible allude to their existence.

We have reasons to think they might have been coterminous, which allows the careful, objective reader to continue the exploration of an original couple who was created innocent *"from the beginning,"* to quote Jesus,[116] again, an eyewitness to the event.

---

116 Matthew 19:4

Appendix III

The Fall of the Angels

The reader should recognize that much of what is commonly accepted as canonical (biblical) regarding the fall of angelic beings, and the interchangeable use of the name Lucifer with that of Satan, is actually extra-biblical development found in the writings of the early Church Fathers.

Lucifer is a combination of two Latin terms: *lux, lucis,* meaning light, and *ferre,* meaning to bring or bear. The original Hebrew in Isaiah 14:12 renders the name *Helel* son of *Shahar.* Both names refer to Babylonian/Canaanite gods: *Helel* was the god of the morning star, and *Shahar* was his father and the god of the dawn. Some theologians are hesitant to attribute the Isaiah passage to a corrupt angel believing it should be applied only to either Sennacherib, king of Assyria, and with it, all of the area of Babylon, or Nebuchadnezzar, who followed as the actual king of Babylon. And further, that the fallen cherub of Ezekiel 28:11-19 should only be applied to the king of Tyre. Others, however, feel that these verses lend themselves to a far larger picture, transcending the arrogance and pride of the named monarchs and that the early Church Fathers were justified in their development of this aspect of Christian diabolism; their thoughts were a plausible understanding of what happened. Jesus refers to Satan as falling from heaven like lightening (Luke 10:18) which is restated in the Revelation of John (12:8-10). Paul's reference to Satan as one masquerading as an "angel of light" (2 Corinthians 11:14) certainly lends itself as having some relationship to the Helel story in Isaiah.

Some things can also be deduced from a purely rational standpoint when coming to grips with a pre-Adamic, angelic fall. An opportunistic and evil personal being was already lying in wait for us in the garden wanting nothing less than our destruction. From whence did he come, and what kind of being was he? Before our creation there was only God and possibly one other rational being: the angels. The early chapters of Job also introduce us to a being intent on our destruction. Satan's name, actually used by Jesus in the Gospel accounts to address the devil during His temptation, was, like Lucifer, originally seen as a role in Hebrew literature: *HaSatan*—the adversary or the accuser. It is employed in this way in the first two chapters of Job. Satan is used for the first time as a proper name, as opposed to the role, in 1 Chronicles 21:1 where Satan causes King David to command an unauthorized census of Israel.

Bibliography

Michael Behe, *Darwin's Black Box: The Biochemical Challenge to Evolution,* New York, Touchstone–Simon and Schuster Inc., 1998.

Michael Behe, *The Edge of Evolution: The Search for the Limits of Darwinism,* New York, Free Press, 2007.

E. Calvin Beisner, *Answers for Atheists, Agnostics, and Other Thoughtful Skeptics: Dialogs about Christian Faith and Life,* Wheaton, IL, Crossway Books, 1993.

Debra Caruso, *The Disappearing Nuclear Family and the Shift to Non-Traditional Households Has Serious Financial Implications for Growing Numbers of Americans,* Huffington Post, January 25, 2013.

Charles Darwin, *The Origin of Species,* sixth edition, Oxford, Oxford University Press, 1998.

Richard Dawkins, "Put Your Money on Evolution," *The New York Times,* April 9, 1989, section VII, p. 35.

Ann Gauger, Douglas Axe and Casey Luskin, *Science and Human Origins,* Seattle, WA, Discovery Institute Press, 2012.

Philip D. Gingerich, "The Whales of Thethys," *Natural History* 103 (April 1994): pp. 86-88.

Stephen Jay Gould, "Hooking Leviathan by Its Past," *Natural History* 103 (May 1994): pp. 8-15.

Richard Lewontin's review of Carl Sagan's *The Demon-Haunted World: Science as a Candle in the Dark*, New York Review of Books, January 9, 1997.

C. S. Lewis, *God in the Dock*, Grand Rapids, MI, William B. Eerdmans Publishing Co., 1973.

C. S. Lewis, *A Grief Observed,* London, Faber and Faber LTD, 1961.

Jacques Maritain, *The Problem of Evil*, Milwaukee, WI, Marquette University Press, 1942.

Kenneth Miller, *Finding Darwin's God: A Scientist's Search for Common Ground between God and Evolution,* New York, HarperCollins, 1999.

New American Standard Bible, Copyright 2006, MacArthur Study Bible, The Lockman Foundation, lockman.org.

George Gaylord Simpson, *The Meaning of Evolution*, revised edition, New Haven, CN, Yale University Press, 1967.

R. C. Sproul, *Reason to Believe: A Response to Common Objections to Christianity*, Grand Rapids, MI, Zondervan Publishing House, 1982.

Jonathan Wells, *The Myth of Junk DNA*, Appendix: The Vitamin C Pseudogene, Seattle, WA, Discovery Institute Press, 2011.

George C. Williams, *The Pony Fish's Glow*, New York, BasicBooks, 1997.

9 781630 470654